Vagus Nerve Basics

A Simple Guide of Natural Methods to Relieve Stress, Restore Ease, and Renew Your Mind-Body Connection

Ione Goodhart

Amuluma Press

© **Copyright Amuluma Press 2022 - All rights reserved.**

The content contained within this book may not be reproduced, duplicated, or transmitted without direct written permission from the author or the publisher.

Under no circumstances will any blame or legal responsibility be held against the publisher, or author, for any damages, reparation, or monetary loss due to the information contained within this book. Either directly or indirectly. You are responsible for your own choices, actions, and results.

Legal Notice:

This book is copyright protected. This book is only for personal use. You cannot amend, distribute, sell, use, quote, or paraphrase any part, or the content within this book, without the consent of the author or publisher.

Disclaimer Notice:

Please note the information contained within this document is for educational and entertainment purposes only. All effort has been executed to present accurate, up-to-date, and reliable, complete information. No warranties of any kind are declared or implied. Readers acknowledge that the author is not engaging in the rendering of legal, financial, medical, or professional advice. The content within this book has been derived from various sources. Please consult a licensed professional before attempting any techniques outlined in this book.

By reading this document, the reader agrees that under no circumstances is the author responsible for any losses, direct or indirect, which are incurred as a result of the use of the information contained within this document, including, but not limited to, — errors, omissions, or inaccuracies.

All rights reserved.

Contents

A Free Gift for You, Dear Reader	1
Introduction	3
1. The Stress Response Cycle	11
2. You've Got Nerve!	35
3. Inner Strength	45
4. Calming Your Mind	60
5. Biofeedback	85
6. Calming Your Body	91
7. The Mind-Body Connection	101
8. Renewing Your Mind-Body Connection	109
Leave a 1-Click Review	114
Conclusion	115
A Free Gift for You, Dear Reader	119
Endnotes	121
Resources	135
Acknowledgments	136
About The Author	137

A Free Gift for You, Dear Reader

Thank you for your purchase. Use this QR code to download the Guide to Stress Management workbook. Or click this link. You'll find:

- Essentials for stress management and stress relief.

- Exercises that help you figure out what holds you back from relieving your stress.

- Prompts for journaling so you can hear your inner wisdom better.

- Easy ways of making simple changes that can help you create better stress management habits.

Introduction

Whenever the human mind perceives a stressful situation, it responds by activating the fight-flight-freeze response from small to large, depending on the situation. This response is a survival mechanism that has existed since ancient times. While much of our body's functional systems have evolved into the present day, this stress response has stayed the same. Sometimes, this stress response is activated more and more in our modern lives. From external stressors, like Covid, climate change, and social injustices, to mention just a few, to other stressors that may exist in our personal lives, like not sleeping well, taking care of an aging parent, or the struggle to pay the bills, and so on, the ongoing stressors and our responses can become a chronic experience. And that stress impacts how we feel, think, and act. You are not alone. In 2022, According to the American Psychological Association in the United States, 27% of adults cannot accomplish what needs to be done, and 37% share that it is hard to do things even when trying because of stress.

Having an acute or chronic health challenge or condition adds to this. It is stressful not to feel well. I spent years addressing a chronic health issue that impacted my nervous system. I felt on edge, sometimes anxious, with panic attacks and migraines—all of which I didn't have before this health diagnosis. If you are going through a health challenge, whatever it may be, reader, my heart goes out to you. Finding compatible doctors and other medical experts who can provide optimal care is also stressful. It requires a significant investment of time and energy. While there are a lot of resources out there, having access to them when needed is sometimes challenging, or the barriers to accessing them make them inaccessible. The last thing you feel like doing when unwell is finding help and resources. In the end, however, if not you, who else? If you want to feel better and improve your wellness, it is generally up to you to be your best health advocate and reach out to receive support. It's about you working towards your health goals, finding the healthcare providers on your healthcare team that are a good match for you, educating yourself on your options, and committing to taking steps towards improved and better health. Do these words resonate with you?

The desire to lead a healthy life with reduced suffering and feel a sense of belonging and connection is a natural human need. Cultivating resilience and feeling good in our bodies and minds helps us be better people. It creates more authentic connections with our loved ones. Having a sense of belonging and relationship starts at home inside of you. It begins with feeling a link to your body even when it is not feeling well. Remembering how to feel good inside your body means feeling mentally and emotionally comfortable with your physical body. And from there, feeling safer and connecting with others. Belonging and connecting to yourself and others creates more happiness.

This book explores non-invasive natural methods that support your body's ability to self-heal your vagus nerve. We begin by understanding the vagus nerve and why it is so essential. Moving forward, we look at methods to reduce suffering and improve your day-to-day experience of life. It is a practical guide to working with the vagus nerve, backed by science. A word about the science piece: the information found in this book is from the research currently available. I've done my best to provide

INTRODUCTION

quality information on the topic of the vagus nerve. References are given in the endnotes and organized by chapter.

Today, I am a dedicated meditator. When I started, the concept of meditation was foreign to me, yet it intrigued me. When I discovered meditation, I was recuperating from burnout. I left my job where I worked a thirteen-hour workday that would usually bleed into the night, five days a week, and often more. When I had weekends, they were spent doing chores and playing catch-up on my personal life, with barely enough time to rest in between, play, or hang out with friends and family. I was not great at saying "no" back then, so I was regularly stuck completing my sensible work within insensible timeframes. Meditation helped me recuperate. I developed better focus and self-care. Eventually, I found a better job that suited me.

A few years later, and unexpectedly, a tiny critter bit me. That bite at that moment, in retrospect, caused a sea-change in my life and what followed was many years of health challenges. A little tick carrying Lyme disease decided I looked like a suitable host and played havoc with my nervous system. I worked with good healthcare professionals who helped my body reduce the bacterial load and neutralize the effects of Lyme that I would live with for the rest of my life. I could not have done it without them. However, they could not help with the aftermath of that bite and the hit my body and the nervous system took.

I'm not a person who gives up. I have deep faith in the healing power of my body, mind, heart, and spirit. I began educating myself. I worked with my doctor and healthcare providers. I consulted other healthcare experts. I called them "My Team." I experienced anger, peak frustration, fatigue, and a tired brain. I fell asleep when I meditated. I cried. I hurt all over; I cycled in and out of negative and positive thoughts and did not give up even though sometimes I wanted to. Throughout it all, I chose to follow what my integrative healthcare providers recommended. In addition, I also tried other complementary approaches, which I also informed my doctors about. I got better. Still, there was room for improvement. It was not until I went to a conference and learned about a part of the nervous system called the "wandering nerve" that I discovered the power of connecting and working with this nerve, my vagus nerve.

I studied my body's neurological system. I learned and used mind-body practices that helped recover my nervous system by supporting this extraordinary vagus nerve. These were crucial and game-changing steps for me on my road to wellness. It has become an essential part of my health path and healing journey. Can you benefit from what I've discovered? I don't know, truthfully. My hope is in sharing this information, you might.

From my experience working with natural methods that support the health of this vagus nerve, I have discovered that the vagus nerve has become my body's superpower. It has helped me be at home in my skin. Perhaps it will be your body's superpower as well. The evidence shows that the vagus nerve is a critical component that helps to counteract the fight-flight-freeze response to the stressors experienced in everyday life. Understanding the role this nerve serves and working with methods that support the health of the vagus nerve may help develop a healthier stress response. In turn, you can become more resilient to stress. When your vagus nerve functions optimally, it reconnects you. It reconnects you to better feelings, clear-headedness, and a sense of belonging. With practice and commitment, you might grow a more profound and pervasive sense of calm.

A strong memory is the first time I sat down to meditate. It was in a tiny, carpeted room, except for myself, my body, my mind, and my being. I followed the meditation steps in a book propped under my knee to keep the pages open. I was shocked by how my mind progressed towards a place of tranquility, and my body began to relax and calm down — I knew I'd chanced upon something monumental for me. My family couldn't understand how simple meditation and a few lifestyle changes made me much calmer and brighter. I was lovingly and annoyingly made fun of because of it. Gradually, I began sharing what I was learning and discovering with friends. I studied more, expanding my knowledge about evidence-based and emerging evidence-informed complementary and integrative health practices. And I experimented with each one to see what worked for me. I did the work. It was hard, and looking back, the journey was worth it. Because now, the result is being able to manage my health proactively. I am well. I have my life back.

A few years ago, I thought, "Why not share this information with others?" Other people have a health challenge and may be looking for natural methods that can support their own personal health journey. I am passionate about holistic health and nature's inherent well-being, which in my humble opinion, supports creating vibrancy in a physical body. This book shares information about essential, simple, natural methods and information geared towards the person who may not feel as well as they wish to. It's organized, so you can use it in a way that works for you. Part 1 is the science and information about the vagus nerve. Part 2 is about the foundational methods I've learned and how-to-do them. These natural methods may help your body's ability to self-heal the vagus nerve, which may help relieve stress, restore ease and renew your mind-body connection. Hopefully, it can be one of the ways that cultivate confidence and faith in the power you have to create better health in your life.

Now, picture this. It is a year from now. You have woken up after eight hours of restful sleep—golden sunlight filters in from your window on a busy little street. You sigh and lean back into your pillow, considering how crisp the morning is. There's heady, sweet tea or coffee brewing downstairs. The scent of it climbs up and wafts into your nose, and you think, "How sweet it is just to be alive." That sentiment, dear reader, is just what we are aiming for.

Part One

Relieve Stress and Renew Your Mind-Body Connection

Science & the Vagus Nerve

> *"If you want to improve the world, start by making people feel safer."* ~ Stephen Porges. Ph.D.

Chapter 1

The Stress Response Cycle

and Polyvagal Theory

FEELING SAFE IS A vital part of enjoying good health. So many of us are in good jobs and doing things that should make us feel content, but we are frequently tense, nervous, worried, or even anxious. Perhaps this is due to several things, like the demands of our profession and the lifestyles we have chosen to live. Perhaps there are struggles in our family, and important relationships or the state of the world worries us. Maybe it's a combination of things. It's tough to feel secure when you are constantly stressed and perhaps frustrated by it, and where the mere sense of safety becomes synonymous with needing to exert yourself more to get it. Your overall health, including mental and emotional health, deserves room to breathe.

Chronic stress affects physical wellness. Think about stress-induced migraines, how stress contributes to obesity, poor lifestyle choices, and age-related illnesses like Alzheimer's and heart disease, anxiety, and depression. Ongoing stress and its components can create insecurity and make us think we are in a perpetual state of danger.

There is a way for us to ground ourselves and work with our bodies to feel safe and secure from the inside out. The ability to do this is through working with our physical body. And the road to get there is a physiological one. When you learn to tune into your body and hear that inner voice inside, you have access to and can actively begin to understand what ways of thinking, feeling, and experiencing are not working for you and what does work for a better, healthier you. A critical path to achieving this state is understanding the Polyvagal theory, which studies the vagus nerve's role in our physical, mental, emotional, and social health and well-being and how this nerve can help you walk up the path to better health.

The Stress Response Cycle

Our entire nervous system, which includes our brain, is nothing short of an ongoing miracle. Lying behind this miracle is an intricate network of millions of cells. You can liken your body's nervous system to a postmaster running the workings of a postal delivery system. It guides almost everything you think, say, feel, or do. Much like receiving mail in your inbox, you don't know all the processes between — from the package being sent to sorting, collecting, analyzing, and delivering. You wait and experience the final result, which is the delivery. Your nervous system is responsible for managing your body, studying different signals from the outside environment that touch your senses, and figuring out, assessing, perceiving, and developing overall awareness. The postmaster, our nervous system, does a brilliant job. It's wonderfully adaptive and cycles through its responsibilities beautifully. And yet the minute you and I are affected by something stressful, the postmaster resorts to shutting down many of its advanced operations and returns to an old way of responding; this is the stress response cycle. Let's take a deeper look at it.

General Overview of the Nervous System

Let's get a picture of the nervous system first to see where the stress response fits. The nervous system has two subsystems— a central one composed of your spinal cord and the brain, called the central nervous system or CNS, and a peripheral one that extends everywhere else, like to and from your arms and legs, called the peripheral nervous system or PNS.

The peripheral subsystem is divided further into the somatic and autonomic nervous systems. The somatic nervous system is responsible for our muscles and outer skin. This system is under our conscious control. The autonomic nervous system is responsible for our inside organs, their systems, and all the related tissues. This system is not under our control.

The autonomic nervous system of ANS is further divided into three anatomical sub-parts. They're called the sympathetic, parasympathetic, and enteric nervous systems.

Sympathetic: The sympathetic nervous system or SNS activates body responses during times of need, mainly when you are in danger or undergoing stress. It is responsible for the body's stress response. The sympathetic nervous system has many vital functions. Among them is preparing our organs to develop an amplified sense of "readiness" whenever trouble is in sight. This process always starts subconsciously. It is automatic and begins without our conscious awareness. Since our body is getting ready to fight the danger or run away from it, we can be reactive.

Parasympathetic: The parasympathetic nervous system or PSNS takes care of the restful and digestive processes which help your body relax, conserve energy and enjoy life. The parasympathetic nervous system has many vital functions opposite the sympathetic nervous system. Among them is to develop a quieting sense of "calming down" after the trouble is gone. Its job is rest, digestion, recreation, and renewal. It is intimately connected to our digestive processes, including the positive, relaxed part of our visits to the bathroom, where everything flows daily and easily, which is why its nickname is the "rest and digest" system. It is also intimately connected to our pleasure and procreative activities, which is why it has another nickname, the "feed, and breed" system.

Enteric: The enteric nervous system, or ENS, controls how your body absorbs and digests food. The enteric system manages activities related to your digestive system, including the flow of materials along your gastrointestinal tract and having an ongoing conversation with your brain, aka your central nervous system. It spans about 30 feet in your body and is connected to your throat (esophagus), your intestines, and all human bodily functions related to the toilet bowl. How well it operates is greatly affected by the sympathetic and parasympathetic aspects. It has a nickname, too. The "second brain."

Stress Cycle Lives Here

The stress response cycle lives in our autonomic nervous system or ANS. This aspect of our nervous system is not under our conscious control. Let's repeat that. It is not under our conscious control. The autonomic nervous system governs involuntary activities of the body, such as heart rate, blood pressure, breathing, digestion, and sexual desire.

The ANS involves the body's complicated processes in seemingly simple ways, such as movement, thinking patterns, and our ability to remember old incidents and process information, which we take for granted. Not to mention more obvious things you do without thinking twice, such as blushing, blinking, and breathing.

Think about it— you don't have to remind yourself to take a breath every second you are alive. That's possible because of your nervous system's ANS. It influences every aspect of the way you function throughout each day of your life. This aspect of the postal delivery system efficiently and fluidly operates moment-to-moment using the entire scope of its miraculous ANS apparatus, including

- Movements, coordination, and balance.

- Sensory perceptions, or how your brain interprets the things you hear, see, touch, taste, and feel,

- Thoughts, learning, and memory.

- Sleep.

- Healing and aging.

- Breathing patterns and heartbeat.

- Responses to a real or perceived threat.

- Digestion and perceptions of thirst and hunger.

- Age-appropriate changes like puberty.

And yet, the minute you and I are affected by something stressful, the alarms go off and signal an emergency. The whole ANS apparatus shifts to the original operating manual, which is ancient. That operating manual is our modern-day stress response cycle. It's also called the fight-flight response or as you will learn, the fight-flight-freeze response.

The History of Fight or Flight Response

Your fight-or-flight response starts in the brain's temporal lobe, very close to your ears. The temporal lobes prioritize and make sense of different electric signals traveling from your sense organs to the mind. The amygdala is part of the temporal lobe and forms memories depending on emotional experiences. Emotional learning occurs in the amygdala, so your understanding of what situations are benign and are not can often be derived from responses based on previous occasions. Because you were almost hit by a car running a red light, your mind automatically thinks that is what will happen again. So, the amygdala wires your responses based on this prior knowledge.

Some of this prior knowledge comes from how our brains evolved. It still has information stored from way back to our human origins in Africa and the way our brain was at that time. That ancient brain is still a part of us today and is also a part of our modern-day response to stress. There was a real need for our ancient ancestors' subconscious reactions to stressors. Imagine you are part of a nomadic group traversing treacherous terrain. Suddenly, you hear the growling of a hungry four-legged predator in the distance. In seconds, it reaches your group and begins making its way to you, one person at a time. Your amygdala forms a core memory at this point. Let's say you run for your life and survive this incident. The next time this same ancestor navigates a terrain remotely similar to the previous one, they may get freaked out for the entire journey until they reach a location where their amygdala perceives they are far enough from the place of "threat," or in other words, a safe place.

Essentially, the first time your ancient ancestor saw the predator and witnessed that horror, their amygdala formed and stored a potent memory. Emotions that include not just how afraid they felt or how horrified they were but the total incident. That lived experience consists of the visuals, the screams, the smells, and the physical ways their body reacted. And their response was to either stop and fight or run away. This is how your fight-or-flight response developed.

Here we are today. This way of storing past information remains with us. Let's say you hear a loud sound. The typically healthy human response is a visceral one sent from your amygdala where that old, core memory is that makes you momentarily alert until you realize it's not a four-legged furry predator, it's a transformer that blew on the electrical line because of the thunderstorm, and then your body begins to calm down.

In our modern world, our nervous system is experiencing ongoing stress regularly. Financial worries every month when the bills become due while taking care of your family and working a full-time job with another part-time gig to help. Perhaps add to that supporting aging parents, the political climate, and the wars in countries where maybe even some of your friends or family are. Time to spend with your friends and social circles, having fun, and doing things you love doesn't seem enough. Over time, when stress overwhelms our body, we can become over-aroused too regularly, which keeps the stress response on without any rest periods. Your nervous system can develop some unhealthy responses, like nervousness, tight muscles, tension in your body, poor breathing, mental worry, and more. In extreme cases, acute or chronic stress responses like anxiety, and mood changes, occur. Or in the case of life-threatening events, hypervigilance, and other symptoms that are a part of disorders related to traumatic s tress.

When you hear a loud sound again, you may feel fear and anxiety pop up. There may be no four-legged predator involved; it's just modern-day life, yet, the amygdala rings alarm bell after alarm bell, and the experience feels like an emergency. That's a state of being where our sole focus is on reacting and fighting off or fleeing the perceived threat before we even pause and think, "But is this worth the trouble?" In this state, the higher centers of our minds, such as the cerebral cortex, are suppressed. We lose our rational abilities to evaluate, mull over and think clearly. Our brains are thrumming to the sounds of "do, do, do" and "act, act, act" over "let's pause and think." Our abilities for precise and accurate organized thinking go out the window, leaving us to act out in crude and stress-inducing patterns that cause reactions.

The Contemporary Understanding of our Nervous System

The traditional understanding of how our autonomic nervous system operates is based on the sympathetic nervous system (SNS), which activates fight-flight responses, and the parasympathetic nervous system (PSNS), which starts the suppressive, calming, and relaxing responses and supports growth, restoration, and digestive responses. The SNS and PSNS complement and oppose each other.

The contemporary understanding of the body's response systems and how they make you act is much more detailed due to recent findings in neuroscience. Dr. Stephen Porges, a pathbreaker in biological psychology, has contributed to delving deeper into why we respond in the ways we do. The polyvagal theory gives a richer view of what the parasympathetic system does, specifically what helps support the rest and digest mode. His theory shares that the parasympathetic system has two subsystems with distinct operational and evolutionary characteristics. And these two subsystems are within the vagus nerve. They are called the *dorsal vagal* and the *ventral vagal* subsystems. Each branch of the vagus nerve uses a perceived threat in a specific way.

The Passive Defense System: Dorsal Vagal Nerve

The PSNS's passive defense system is the dorsal vagus nerve. It is a primitive nerve common to all animals (including fish); the dorsal vagus travels down the spine, controlling the function of our lungs, hearts, and stomach. It moderates heartbeats, prevents them from becoming too rapid or erratic and aids essential processes like digestion. Under normal circumstances, the dorsal vagus clamps down on the impulsive actions of the SNS. It brings the PSNS's "rest and digest" "feed-and-breed" system into play. It helps you go from a state of arousal (the SNS) to one where you are calm and relaxed (the PSNS). Essentially, its functions are positive and help you retain a sense of equilibrium, especially after something has happened to upset it. It helps your body move between stimulation and relaxation, so neither becomes excessive. Sometimes, when the SNS is too aroused, the dorsal vagus can push the entire system into a "frozen state," where you feel like a deer caught in the headlights. Ever felt like that before?

Imagine a hypothetical scenario of our friend, Susan. She is in a tiny elevator, stuck for a moment. It smells old and stale. There's no fan. The walls are dark-colored and gray, and there's very little light. It is mostly dark. The first response happens via the SNS, which takes her through all the stages of being alarmed. Some signs that she's moving into a stress response are rapid heartbeat, breathing difficulties, dilated pupils, high blood pressure, and body chills. She is unaware that her body is mobilizing this response, causing a cascading series of bodily changes because it all happens automatically and unconsciously. She may or may not begin to notice the aftermath: she is suddenly breathing differently and feeling aroused/alert/stressed. After some time, the PSNS's dorsal vagal system activates itself. It slows down Susan's heart rate and reduces her blood pressure. This is if everything is happening in a balanced way. Instead, suppose the dorsal vagal response to calm Susan is too severe. In that case, it can suppress her heartbeats (with the benign intention of slowing them down) to a place where she may faint or go into shock or, at the most extreme, induce a stroke (generally when issues like poor cardiac health are present).

Susan survives. She gets out of the elevator unharmed. Her amygdala builds a compelling memory of the interiors of the elevator (the dark gray walls, the darkness, the musty smell) and everything that made it so terrifying. This memory gets shelved beyond the realm of her conscious awareness. She takes a deep breath, shakes her body, and moves on with her life. One day, her boss asks her to come to a meeting. The moment she enters the meeting room, the alarm bells go off because her eyes notice the walls are the same shade of gray as the elevator's walls. But she is unaware of the connection between the color of the meeting room's walls and the elevator walls. Her subconscious memory, however, does. Instead, all she notices is that she begins to feel alert and alarmed. Her PSNS's dorsal vagal nerve is activated, sending her body into a "freeze" mode. She feels that she is not fully present. She realizes she cannot think or say a single logical thing. She feels stuck. That's because the front part of her brain is physiologically inaccessible. She wonders what's going on and cannot participate in the meeting. She begins to take deep breaths and can move to the restroom. The act of walking and breathing helps the front part of her brain turn back on. She feels better, and she returns to her office surroundings.

If this response repeats itself enough, Susan may find ways to forget by picking up habits to cope with it. Sometimes it may be poor coping habits, like emotional eating, drinking alcohol, smoking, or watching excessive TV. She may begin to distance herself from her loved ones because she cannot think or function well without getting stressed by something as seemingly ordinary as a gray wall or a small room. Her stress response cycle is stuck in alarm mode. There's hope, however, for Susan. There is a way for Susan to listen to her body's signals and re-learn how to respond better.

The Social Engagement System: Ventral Vagal

The PSNS's social engagement system is the ventral vagal nerve. This subsystem connects the brain to your heart, lungs, and other organs above the diaphragm. It forms the core of your nature as a social being and is a big part of being in relationships with people.

Since the early days of neuroanatomy, it has been widely known that the autonomic nervous system or ANS has nerve fibers responsible for transmitting information from the body to the brain. According to polyvagal theory, human facial expressions reflect physical reactions resulting from these transmission exchanges. In other words, you can form an understanding of a person's internal state based on their facial expressions.

Imagine you are facing someone with the most unpleasant facial expressions. Their brows are all scrunched, they're frowning as if you have done something nasty to them, and no matter how cooperative you try to be, nothing you say or do elicits a smile. You may think, "Wow, what a prude!" but you don't know that this person is suffering from a big case of worry brought on by their ventral vagal system.

Interestingly, you can observe the ventral vagus at work through face-to-face communication. The face is how you portray any internal threat you feel. So, let's say you are talking to Susan, who was stuck in that elevator. You are wearing a gray suit, and it looks great on you. Unknown to you, it manages to evoke unpleasant memories in Susan. The result is a face that conveys a message you interpret as her just wanting to run as far as she can from you.

Unpleasant facial expressions symbolize that the ventral vagal subsystem is functioning at a subpar level. On the other hand, when the ventral vagal system is working well, we respond by showing what we feel— centered, safe and secure. We smile and maintain eye contact while also speaking in even tones. Everything about our posture shows we are relaxed and feel secure and confident. When our mind isn't spread across a million irrelevant things, we also hear what's being said better.

Here's an example. Think of a baby who hears a mother sing and falls asleep or a father who reads bedtime stories to his child. The child's face shows how they feel. They are relaxed, content, and about to nod off. When this happens, a little powerhouse of a gland gets turned on, and the child's sense of feeling physically safe occurs. This is the pituitary gland which secretes a neurotransmitter called oxytocin. Oxytocin reduces tension and anxiety and is often associated with a feel-good high. Trust, empathy, gazing, pleasant recollections, bonding, and constructive communication are positive emotional reactions and pro-social behaviors that oxytocin influences.

The PSNS's ventral vagal subsystem is the mediator affecting all your social relationships. When you see something that makes you happy, your face reflects your calmness and security. And when you encounter something that leaves an unpleasant internal response, your face, voice, and gestures will portray your discomfort.

The Dangers Of Chronic Stress

Each person has different ways of outwardly responding to stress, even though the biological process works the same inside our bodies. Stressors in life are about as perennial as the air we breathe. The threat-response system can overexert itself when encountering situations, people, or things that make us feel nervous or on edge. As a result, we experience chronic stress, the constant feeling of being tired, worried, and frustrated, which can hurt our health if left unchecked.

Chronic stress results when the body experiences stressors with increased intensity and frequency— so much so that the ANS slowly loses the ability to induce the body's ability to relax. The body remains in a chronic state of arousal. What are stressors? Stressors are those situations and things you consider threats to you, your life, and your loved ones. Stressors can appear worse if you also think your resources to handle them are small compared to how big they feel. When you cross swords with a stressor, your body's threat response system is turned on.

How you think about those stressors in your life influences your experience. This increases or decreases the intensity of your stress response, your fight-flight-freeze response. Your stress cycle is your body's physiological response that either compels you to run, fight, or freeze, and it happens automatically. However, when you have regular, ongoing stressors in your life, without managing how they make you feel, you might be inclined to get stressed more quickly. Haven't you had insignificant situations happen to you, yet they can feel like significant stressors? These could include your job's demands, minor conflicts in your relationship, the coffee being too bitter in the morning, waking up fifty minutes before the alarm goes off, and being unable to fall back asleep.

It's worth mentioning that humans are adept at handling acute stress because it is short-lived and demands an immediate response. Once the threat is gone, we automatically calm down until something of equal or greater acuteness happens. But in chronic stress, which is steady over extended periods, your body's nervous system gets used to being "on" all the time which our conscious awareness notices as feeling "worried" or "on edge." This becomes a cycle where your mind constantly looks for "upsetting" situations or things. Once you are on this cycle, stepping off or slowing down becomes one of your biggest challenges.

Let's go back to our friend Susan. Impacted by chronic stress, Susan calls and tells you she isn't getting paid for her freelancing work. She is highly apprehensive about the situation. You do your best to comfort her and tell her she will get paid. A week goes by, and she calls once again and says she has finally received her payment, but now (as in seconds after receiving her compensation), she is worried that the company won't give her any more work because she had left them so many messages. She's started to worry about how her boss perceives her actions, affecting how she feels in the moment. She worried about her future. Her nervous system is responding to her chronic stressed state, and her mind is now worried about what will happen.

Chronic stress impacts both the body and the mind. It produces psychological and physical symptoms that can keep you from doing routine things and create nervousness even when completing simple tasks. Some of the common signs include:

- Body pains and aches.

- Insomnia.

- Brain fog.

- Fatigue.

- Loss of control.

- Helplessness and anger.

- Lowered immunity and greater frequency of illnesses.

- Nervousness.

- Irritability.

- Stress migraines.

- Gastrointestinal imbalances.

How do you know if your stress is chronic? There are some signs to look for. For most, when chronic stress is present, it has already been around for a while and is a part of our pattern of living. As humans, we know how to adapt. We learn to live with chronic stress as a fixture, thinking it is normal, but it is not. Read the following questions below. Do they leave you feeling like this sounds like your situation right now?

- Do you feel moody or irritated without any discernible reason at times?

- Does it always feel like you are worrying about things?

- Do you have zero time in your day for self-care and relaxation?

- Do you turn to harmful ways of coping mechanisms (smoking, alcohol, and the like) to numb your thoughts?

- Do minor stressors overwhelm you?

Our modern lifestyles, while becoming increasingly convenient, contribute to chronic stress. Loneliness, high-pressure jobs, heavy traffic, and the need to prove ourselves for external validation can keep our bodies on alert. The fight-flight-freeze response that was designed to help in life-threatening situations is always ready to be activated. Whether it is quickly running to cross a road if the green walking signal turns red too soon or swerving to avoid a speeding car or it was a second in the day when your boss told you to write a report in twenty-four hours. When activated regularly without rest, it wears us down, and we can experience emotional and physical weakness over time. Our bodies were designed for cycling through the stress response, not being stuck in it.

Fortunately, we can heal our bodies from the effects of stress. It takes time, patience, and some faith and trust in yourself. Of course, any changes you make to your lifestyle— especially those that take work in reorienting your mindset— will demand time and commitment, but what good positive change in life doesn't? Most things worth having take effort because the transition you go through to become a better you is as important as the end goal.

The Polyvagal Theory, In a Nutshell

Dr. Porges has shown that the two branches of the vagal nerve serve different purposes and relate to how the threat response system evolved. A primitive addition, the passive defense system, leads to immobilization behaviors— for instance, feigning death if that is essential for survival. The more evolved branch, the social engagement system, is tied to self-soothing and social communication behaviors. Porges believes these different functions grew out of the evolution of our nervous system from a common ancestor in the deep history of our nervous system. The brain's oldest or most primitive pathways are only active when the newer or more recently evolved ones fail. The latest pathway, social engagement, is the one that supports social communication and self-regulation. When the newest one is on, it helps balance the overall autonomic state. This manages how people express emotions and interact with others. What's happening inside the body dictates behaviors, actions, words, and expressions. In short, your responses.

This is a new understanding of how the entire nervous system works. And with that, it gives us incredible implications for how to work with and better manage the body and the brain and understand ourselves and other people's bodies and brains in ways that might seem impossible.

Let's put it all together. What is the autonomic nervous system? It's the automatic responses that happen at an unconscious level using the SNS and PSNS of the ANS.

These are things you can't consciously control. You don't exactly think, "I want my lungs to pump air," or "I want my stomach to digest food," for these processes to happen. They happen independently; if they didn't, living would be impossible. The essential role your ANS plays is keeping you alive and feeling good. Once again, if you traverse back to prehistoric times, you can't overthink and make conscious decisions whenever you encounter a life-threatening issue. You have to act as quickly and reflexively as possible, which by necessity means your response will be unconscious and automatic. So the body forms an energy resource balance that allows you to use extra energy for these automatic responses and conserve energy when you are relatively safe.

Neuroception

The body has an unconscious ability to scan the world around you and perceive signs that tell it that there is incoming danger. Conversely, it can also interpret that all is safe. So, your body tells you to walk quickly when you come to a crossing. And it tells you to slow down once you've crossed the road. You don't need to "consciously" think before carrying out these actions. These abilities enable your nervous system to influence your response without consciously thinking about it. This is called *neuroception.*

Seth Porges offers a simple way to understand neuroception. It's like an inner traffic light. Your neuroception will look a person up and down and ask: "Are they safe or not?" It is a force potent enough to control our bodies and induce responses we are not consciously formulating. When you see someone who makes your neuroception go, "Hey, they have a good vibe," the green light state is automatically activated. You feel safe and warm, and your heart rate remains or goes down till it is even. Your saliva and digestion become stimulated— which is why we often feel hungry when in good company. Your facial muscles become friendly and relaxed, so your emotions come through when you talk to people. You can maintain eye contact without your hands trembling. Tiny muscles in the mid-ear regions activate within your head, allowing you to pick up frequencies connected with the human voice. So, when you perceive safety, you can make out sounds and words of people talking even if you are in a crowded space.

Next, let us say you see someone and your neuroception goes, "Hold up, I don't know how I feel about this person." This is the yellow light, and you feel a sense of impending anticipation— although it's not entirely pervasive. "Oh, there is something off here with this person." Your body starts going into a warning mode where you might respond by withholding information and changing how you present yourself. Your heartbeats increase, and you get a resting emotionless face. The middle ear muscles shut down, meaning you no longer hear those vibrations associated with human speech. These vibrations are the mid-range level range of sounds.

Instead, you pick up on very low and high frequencies, called predator sounds. The more these sounds grow, the closer you get to the red light, where your neuroception is full-on telling you that the person or situation is absolutely and unequivocally not good for you or dangerous. You actively think spending a second longer with them is not a good idea. Your response may be a fight, flight, or freeze. You feel the impulse to defend yourself, walk away, or can't move and stay rooted to the spot.

Neuroception is tricky, too. Today, because of our ancient ancestors, our body's nervous system has evolved in a way where there is a bias toward locating danger, even if it may not be present. This means we can rely too much on our neuroception and make unconscious on-the-spot decisions not based on any real threat, yet it still causes a stress response. Let's say you meet someone who matches your vibe, and your neuroception goes, "Hey, cool human. I would like to know them better." That is fine. They say something, and then you think quietly, "Um, what was that?" You feel like something's off. You wonder if they have your best interest in mind. It would not be the first time you mistrusted someone or a situation, right?

Another important aspect is that the nervous system's underlying functional neural pathways always determine the traffic light states and responses— green, yellow, and red- *in the order of evolution*. So, the more danger your neuroception perceives, the more primitive your response. It makes sense— you are just looking to survive here, and all higher thinking has gone out the window. There is no fighting between these states to find a champion that will go to the ANS and get it to announce, "hey, we have a winner, and it is the yellow light state," in your mind. Instead, if you find your first response is to shut down and freeze completely, you *know* the red light is on. This is essentially your most reptilian response. By the way, when reptiles face a threat, they do not flee or fight. They play dead. Humans and other mammals likewise freeze when they face the same threat perceptions.

There is nothing wrong with a healthy balance between these states. It's a cycle! You see, we cannot be in a perennial state of relaxation. A green light state is a place of rest and recovery where we prepare ourselves for transitioning into the yellow light state and back. At times we feel more alert in the red and then back to yellow, and so on, based on the ANS's determination.

Susan is back in college and has a critical test in a week. She has taken the time to prepare, but this week is the make-or-break time for her. Her apprehension is at a natural high, compelling her to sift through copious amounts of study material with increased focus and concentration. Susan's mind is focused on getting over what is coming— that is, the test— with success. Now, if her nervous system can transition between the yellow and green light states healthily, this is as far as it goes. The anxiety she feels dissipates after the examination ends, and she slowly calms down and goes into conservation mode.

If her responses are stressed and hyperactive, she may enter the red-light state at any point in time, and when she does, she stops being able to think. Have you ever faced a situation where something important is happening, and you know you need to answer or speak to succeed— but you have entirely frozen? Susan is back now, only this time, she's a little older and appearing for another exam. She has spent months studying, perhaps much too hard, until she cannot sleep or function normally. On the test day, despite how much time and care she has taken, she becomes overwhelmed, blanks out, and breaks down. Eventually, she goes home without answering a single question. The question paper looks like a swimming haze to her confused eyes, and she can't understand what any of the options mean. She's in the red light state.

Susan had a pretty tough childhood. Much expectation rested on her acing every exam with a clean A. Her mother always told her, "You're not doing your best! Try harder! You can't disappoint us! Your father spent so much on your education!" On exam day, the benign, kind proctor told the class, "Do your best." Still, Susan's nervous system interpreted those words as being connected to her parent's expectations, invoking unpleasant and upsetting memories that were difficult for her and led to what followed during the exam. So, essentially we all dip into the red light, but some dip into it more regularly and have a more difficult time returning to the calm of the green light state. Additionally, people who have experienced a real threat to life, witnessed others being harmed, and have had other repeated encounters that were emotionally and/or physically harmful can be traumatized. All trauma exists in this red zone.

Painful incidents repeated over time or life-threatening events can leave a mark on the nervous system of those who have had them. Trauma is a vitally important topic and beyond the scope of this book. If you feel you have had trauma in your life, please reach out to a trained professional. They can help you heal from it and support you in recovering.

Self-Healing

Returning your nervous system to better health is possible. Learning to work with the vagus nerve can support improved health and well-being. To think something so small could impact so much. The vagus nerve's job is to send information to every organ system about whether a situation or person is safe or dangerous. The organ system will then respond depending on the kind of information the vagus nerve carries. The message on the harmful and hazardous side regularly contributes to how much stress is in our daily lives. This might not sound very good, and yet there's hope. So, yes, you cannot control your digestion, heart rate, pulse, or even the way your hands tremble. However, there happens to be one essential thing you can regain control over that helps all your systems that fall under the ANS. Do you know what it is? *It is your breathing.*

While your respiratory system makes your breath happen without conscious thought because it's a part of the ANS. Your somatic nervous system **is** under your conscious control. The somatic system controls your muscles and movement. So, dear reader, you can move your muscles that control how deep or shallow your breath is. How much air you bring into your body or take out of your body is still in the realm of your conscious thinking and awareness. The act of movement is always at your disposal, is always conscious, and is *in your control*. For real, it is powerful. When you decide to move your muscles to change your breathing rate, irrespective of what color the traffic light signals to your vagus nerve, you begin to gently move your inner traffic light to green.

When you learn to put your heart and soul into remembering to move through breathe at those stressful moments, the vagus nerve will link your respiratory patterns to everything else. Sensors in your lungs automatically slow your heartbeat when your breathing slows down. Conversely, when you breathe too fast, your heartbeat automatically increases. Dr. Porges says the key lies in focusing on your breathing. Let's say that again: the key lies in focusing on your breathing. When you breathe, your body moves. Breathing is movement. Deep breathing matters. Breathing well matters.

Any movement matters when it comes to changing our stress response. Physical activity signals your brain that you have successfully overcome a threat. When your brain knows this, it will begin to give you the comfort of your body returning to a safe harbor, a shelter, and a refuge. Breathing consciously, of course, is choosing a movement. By the way, if you add another movement to your conscious breathing, it becomes a dynamic duo. Interestingly, it does not have to be a big movement, either. You can move your arm. You can shake your head. You can hug yourself. Or you can take a walk, go exercise, do a few jumping jacks. You get the point. Physical activity is the singularly most efficient route to move through the stress response cycle. This is empowering.

Polyvagal Theory in Contemporary Healthcare

This theory is making essential changes to healthcare. Understanding the polyvagal theory helps people mold their nervous system into building a stronger sense of safety. If you are experiencing that fight-flight-freeze response like a sense of disconnection or separateness, feeling numb or shut down, overwhelmed, over-aroused or overworked, the way forward is to move, to take action. The way out is to move towards a sense of safety. Once your body realizes you are safe, it will transition into the social engagement system.

It can help in a deeper understanding of the effect of trauma on the body and its response to it. For health conditions, understanding Polyvagal therapy can help people re-pattern their nervous system to manage their pain and suffering better—especially physical conditions involving pain and the gastrointestinal areas. Research has shown that these issues are much more prevalent in people who have suffered from trauma and physical abuse. Diseases like fibromyalgia and irritable bowel syndrome are poorly understood in terms of pathophysiology, and research into chronic autonomic response may find different answers.

In support of mental health, working with awareness of polyvagal theory is particularly beneficial. In therapy disciplines like dialectical behavior therapy (DBT) and cognitive behavior therapy (CBT), the focus is on thought-restructuring practices that help individuals shift from a state of separateness and disconnection by assisting them to return to the present, the here and now, and with that, cultivate self-realization. By learning to be in the present moment, you can become aware of the tension in your body. With that awareness, you organically wake up from the inner thoughts and feelings, keeping the fight-flight-freeze response occurring. In another therapy, Motivational interviewing (MI) actively relies on reflective listening and mirroring. The counselor reflects the patient's thoughts and answers them in a way that makes them think, "Oh, now I see what I'm doing." The patient comes to a healthy realization about coping solutions *by themselves in the present moment.* It can also assist in creating stronger ties to feelings of safety.

Therapy and counseling assist in creating stronger ties to feelings of safety. For those who have experienced traumatizing events, polyvagal theory has enhanced an understanding of how to help people recover and heal. A healthy, compassionate counselor and therapist who practices self-care is a provider whose vagus nerve operates very well. A client working with a therapist can experience what it can be like to be with another person and share a safe, positive therapeutic connection in a healing environment. They relearn the green light effect of their nervous system, and what feeling safe can be like with a trained professional who is a safe person. The relationship becomes a pathway to developing more ease in their personal life and socializing with others. It teaches them the core realities of feeling safe and learning about belonging and connection.

My Reflections & Notes

In the next chapter, you will learn more about your nervous system. For now, what did you learn about the stress response cycle? What parts of this chapter resonated with you?

Chapter 2

You've Got Nerve!

Becoming Comfortable With Your Autonomic Nervous System

Your body is an amazingly complex structure that does far more than you think. Each day, your nervous system, vagus nerve, organs, muscles, bones, senses, and more work together to achieve impressive feats so you can live and thrive.

A New Meaning to You've Got Nerve!

Remember the song *Shake Them Skeleton Bones* by The Kiboomers, where certain bones are connected to other bones? This song, in particular, strikes a cord because it speaks of the connection between the bones of your body which join together to form one skeleton.

Let's sing the same about your nervous system. You already know that your nervous system is vital in almost everything your body does. It influences every communication, movement, and process carried out by your body and every resulting sensation you experience. It is only natural that if a part of this undergoes damage by an illness or injury, the whole suffers in terms of function and effective communication.

Consider your local mail system or package delivery service. You have a postal delivery service that brings mail to the convenience of your doorstep from different mail systems. The postal delivery system always arranges and sorts the mail to ensure you don't end up with someone else's package. Similarly, your senses (touch, sight, taste, smell, and hearing) take in messages (envelopes or boxes) from the world around you. These messages travel through your nerves, much like mail from different parts of the world reach you. Finally, your brain acts as the sorting center that decides which mail belongs to you and which should be discarded because it is irrelevant.

The nervous system contains more than seven trillion nerves that transmit signals to and from the brain, spinal cord, and the rest of your body. Approximately eighty-six billion nerves in the brain extend to the very end of your extremities. For example, there are an impressive seven thousand nerves in each foot and three thousand in each fingertip. The nervous system is vast and very complex. For ease of understanding, let's break it down into tiny bits of information necessary to the vagus nerve. Why is this important? Perhaps learning the fundamentals will help you with the natural methods shared later in this book. It also gives you a foundation to stand on as you build new ways of feeling better and improving your health.

What Does the Nervous System Control?

Your nervous system has three main parts: the central nervous system (CNS), the peripheral nervous system (PNS), and the autonomic nervous system (ANS). Each component or system (while having an independent function) also works with the others to control everything from breathing and speaking to moving and swallowing.

The Central Nervous System

Your central nervous system (CNS) has two distinct parts: the spinal cord and the encephalon. The encephalon combines several components— like your cerebellum, thalamic structure, brain stem, and brain. They work as a unit. Our bodies depend on the brain to perform vital functions each day. Within this network of brilliance, billions of neurons perpetually operate and control functions like breathing, walking, and everything in between. The thalamus and other structures connected to the brain are responsible for receiving messages sent from the cerebrum and transmitting them to the rest of the body. Remember the mail analogy from earlier? The thalamus plays a notable role in sorting and forwarding messages where they need to go. Many of the information threads traveling from the egg-shaped structure are complex. They relate primarily to your abilities of sense and touch. These messages also play a vital role in helping you gauge emotions like hunger.

Your brain stem connects the brain to the spinal cord. Attached to the thalamus is the cerebellum, which coordinates movement. It is also home to the neurons controlling life-sustaining functions such as heart rate, breathing, and consciousness. Your spinal cord exists outside your skull. Your spinal cord lies within a canal that runs down your back. The spinal column is a channel that extends from the base of your head at the brain stem down the center of your back to the bottom near your tailbone. The spinal cord is composed of nerves that send and receive messages to and from your brain. The information sent between your brain and spinal cord controls virtually every function and sensation in your body.

The Peripheral Nervous System

The peripheral nervous system has two parts, the somatic and autonomic. Your peripheral nervous system (PNS) is where you will find the cranial nerves, the nerve roots of your spinal cord, and other nerves that extend from your spinal cord to your extremities. Each cranial nerve has one of three roles. The nerve either controls motor function (movement) and your ability to sense things or helps you feel pain by transmitting pain messages to the brain.

The Somatic Nervous System

The somatic nervous system is responsible for the intentional movements of the skeletal muscles. For instance, when you get up from the dining chair where you are eating to walk to the kitchen, these movements are intentional. You consciously think you want to stand up and actively decide which direction to go, so one foot is put in front of the other as you walk to another room.

The Autonomic Nervous System

The autonomic nervous system, or ANS, controls your body's functions and daily activities without consciously thinking about them. Breathing, digesting, metabolizing, and regulating your body temperature are examples of your autonomic nervous system's functioning. Two-component parts— the sympathetic nervous system and the parasympathetic nervous system make up the ANS. Both the sympathetic nervous system, or SNS, and the parasympathetic nervous system, or PSNS, are active in stress and relaxation. Your SNS, when activated, is responsible for your body' s fight-flight-freeze response. Conversely, when activated, the PSNS controls the "rest and digest response."

The Sympathetic Nervous System

Your SNS's job is to scan for perceived threats and turn on the threat response system, your fight-flight-freeze response. Your sympathetic nervous system may prevent the body from performing specific tasks until the stress has passed. For example, you may be unable to digest in fight-flight-freeze mode. Your immune system may also weaken. Have you noticed how when you sense fear or apprehension, your pupils increase in size and your heart rate increases, and you may experience other temporary changes in your body?

Specific chemicals called epinephrine and norepinephrine get released into your body. These chemicals help your body protect itself when it feels like it is under attack or in danger. For example, rather than focusing on digesting food, it will be more beneficial if your heart is pumping faster in case you need to run away from a pressing threat.

The Parasympathetic Nervous System

The PSNS functions when the SNS is calm. The PSNS is responsible for your body's functions when it is in a state of rest. The PSNS changes several body functions to help it recover from a stressor or traumatic experience. In most cases, these functions are the opposite of what happens when your SNS is activated. For example, your parasympathetic nervous system will stimulate your digestive and immune systems. It helps you go from a state of heightened alert to your pupils decreasing in size, your heart rate slowing, and your lungs returning to a "normal" state where you feel calmer. These processes help your body rest, recover, and focus on maintaining your health and wellness.

Remember that an experience does not have to be life or death for the SNS to activate. Other emotional, day-to-day experiences can turn on your threat response system. When you try presenting to a group of people, are you aware of the body sensations you experience? For example, how do you feel about public speaking? How you feel may differ from someone more comfortable with public speaking. Are you afraid of getting on an airplane? Similarly, if you fear flying and have to board a flight, sense how your body prepares to protect itself from perceived danger.

The vagus nerve is a part of the PSNS. It is a diverse, essential nerve that provides sensory and motor function to several body parts, including your ears, throat, internal organs, and tongue. The vagus nerve has the most extended pathway of any cranial nerve beginning at the base of your head at your brainstem and extending into your stomach.

What is the Vagus Nerve?

Vagus is the Latin term for wandering, which is well suited to the path the vagus nerve takes through your body. Your vagus nerve is not only the longest of the cranial nerves but the most complex. While most cranial nerves connect to various areas of the head and neck, the vagus nerve also connects to the organs of the abdomen and chest.

The vagus nerve leaves the brain at a part of the brainstem called the medulla oblongata. The vagus nerve then travels from the base of your skull down through your neck. It travels between the carotid artery, the significant artery where you can feel your pulse in your neck, and your internal jugular vein. The internal jugular vein is another large vein in the neck that is more difficult to feel.

At this point, the right and left vagus nerve go their separate ways. The left vagus nerve travels in front of your heart, behind your left lung, and into your esophagus before traveling to your abdomen.

The right vagus nerve passes behind your esophagus and right lung before joining the left vagus in your stomach, which eventually ends in the colon. The vagus nerve has branches that travel from the main nerve to various areas throughout your chest and abdominal cavity. The vagus nerves stimulate parts of your ear, throat, larynx, esophagus, lungs, trachea, heart, and digestive tract.

Your vagus nerve plays a crucial role in many internal organ functions, including heart rate, digestion, cardiovascular activity, breathing, and other reflex actions such as swallowing, sneezing, coughing, and vomiting.

The Role of Nerves and Your Physical Health

Your central nervous system is your body's primary command center. Much like a postman guiding the mail delivery so that you get what is yours and not your neighbors', your central nervous system shows almost every function and process in your body, including those you can and cannot control. Your nervous system can affect every aspect of your health, including physical illness. Because your nerves travel throughout your entire body, it is easy to imagine many potential conditions or disorders that could affect your nerves.

Disease

Infections such as cancers and autoimmune disorders (e.g., rheumatoid arthritis, lupus, diabetes) can lead to nerve damage. Diabetes, for example, can lead to a condition called neuropathy which causes pain and tingling in the legs and feet.

Accidental Injury

Specific injuries can cut, stretch, or crush your nerves. You could lose sensation in a particular body area due to nerve damage depending on the injury's extent. When a nerve is injured or damaged, it cannot function as it needs to. The nerve may be slow to send or receive messages, or it may not send or receive communication at all. Nerve injuries can cause physical sensations such as pain, tingling, numbness, or "pins and needles." There are several possible sources of nerve damage.

Stroke

Strokes occur when one of your brain's blood vessels becomes blocked or ruptures. When this happens, that brain area cannot get enough blood to send or receive messages through the nervous system. Nerve damage from a stroke can range from mild to very severe.

Pressure

When a nerve is compressed or pinched, it does not get enough blood to live or do its job correctly. Common reasons nerves are pinched include overuse, structural problems (problems with your joints), and tumors. Like a disease, when the nerve does not get enough blood to function correctly, it can cause pain, numbness, and tingling in various body areas.

Aging

With age, the speed at which your nervous system communicates begins to slow. Signals may not travel as quickly or effectively as they used to. This can lead to weakness and slower reflexes. You may also notice reduced or lost sensations in your fingers and toes.

Toxic Substances

Certain drugs, including prescription medications, can cause peripheral neuropathy (nerve damage).

Cranial Nerve Disorder

Injury or damage to one or more of your cranial nerves is called cranial nerve disorder. When you experience cranial nerve problems, it can lead to reduced sensation or pain in specific body areas. General symptoms you may notice if you have cranial nerve disorder include vertigo, hearing loss, paralysis, and weakness. You may also discern your sense of smell and taste is off, and you may struggle to swallow or produce certain facial expressions.

The Role of Nerves and Your Mental Health

Your brain and nervous system are vital in maintaining your mental health. Mental health challenges and conditions negatively affect your thoughts, emotions, and behaviors. Certain conditions, such as bipolar disorder, depression, and anxiety, create imbalances in certain neurotransmitters in your brain.

These imbalances affect how the cells and nerves in your central nervous system and other parts of your nervous system communicate. When this happens, your brain may not send the proper (or any) communication or instructions to your body. As a consequence, the lack of communication, in turn, can lead to new or worsening mental illness.

My Reflections & Notes

In the next chapter, you will learn more about your vagal tone. This information will be a foundation for your chosen holistic ways to relieve stress, restore ease and renew your body-mind connection. For now, what areas of your health do you want to improve? Be honest with yourself. Use the space below to journal areas of your health that you *want to improve*. Maybe you'd like more internal peace, freedom from chronic anxiety and high blood pressure, or a break from being overcommitted. Pen all of it down.

These are the areas of my health I want to improve:

Chapter 3

Inner Strength

Testing Your Vagus Nerve

Let's begin by going back to Susan. It is a sunny morning. Susan has just woken up. Birds are chirping, and she lays in bed for a second, wondering what she will do on such a lovely day. She instinctively feels she should relax and wind down from the busy week. Perhaps get some coffee? Or maybe read a book for a bit? Or maybe check the laptop and peak to see if any work emails have come in, although it's a Saturday? Against the nagging "No, I'm not working on a Saturday" thoughts in her mind, she tells herself, "Eh, it can't hurt just to take a look."

She opens her laptop and catches an urgent email from her supervisor. Suddenly, the sunny morning goes right out the window. She gets hit by a wave of stress. She immediately feels how pressured she is about her work and how mentally stretched and exhausted she is daily. She lies in bed and closes her eyes, but sleep won't come. There's the realization that she won't have any time for herself, and the rest of her Saturday will be spent thinking about her job responsibilities. It's not a great way to spend the weekend.

While Susan is busy focusing on how the stress from her email is about to ruin her weekend, she has no idea how it works as a silent torturer inside her body. Research states that chronic stress contributes to chronic inflammation, which harms you. Chronic inflammation contributes to cardiovascular dysfunctions, cancers, autoimmune diseases, lifestyle illnesses like Type 2 Diabetes, and mental health issues such as depression and pervasive anxiety disorders. Over time, chronic stress can alter brain structure and lead to the premature death of vital neurons, reducing your cognitive ability to think and function optimally.

Research shows that the vagus nerve is *crucial* in addressing chronic stress. An essential aspect of your vagus nerve is its' vagal tone. Simply speaking, the vagal tone indicates how strong your vagus nerve is. Vagal tone is often used to evaluate cardiac function, but it's also informative for gauging emotional control and other processes affected by the parasympathetic activity of your PSNS.

"Tone" refers to the vagus nerve's constant, low-level parasympathetic function. Remember, this is the calming part of your nervous system. The vagus nerve is vital in reducing heart rate, gland activity in the heart, lungs, digestive tract, and liver. It's also vital in regulating the immune system, controlling gastrointestinal sensitivity, and preventing inflammation. The amount of stimulation the vagus nerve provides is adjusted by how the sympathetic and parasympathetic branches of the autonomic nervous system work together.

Since the vagus nerve controls your heart rate and breathing rate, learning whether or not you have a high or low vagal tone can provide a snapshot of your overall health. A high vagal tone is linked to happiness, security, and balance in your body which is the physiological state of homeostasis. One study discovered a lower incidence of stroke, diabetes, and cardiovascular disease in those with high vagal tone. Conversely, a low tone is linked to a depressed mood, stress, and a lack of focus. Low vagal tone also can indicate poor cognitive and emotional regulation.

Testing your Vagal Tone

How is vagal tone tested? Typically, it is checked with an electrocardiogram, also called an ECG, in a doctor's office. An ECG measures heartbeat patterns. When you take a deep breath in, your heart rate increases so that more oxygenated blood can be sent to your body's tissues and organs. The exhalation phase of breathing is associated with a reduced heart rate. You'll need to visit your doctor to check your vagal tone with an ECG.

The vagus nerve controls heart rate variability (HRV). This is the heart's capacity to respond to change. Reduced heart rate and enhanced HRV are common effects of a raised vagal tone. In addition, there are individual differences in a vagal tone; over the lifespan, the vagal response naturally changes and diminishes with age.

You can, however, test your vagal tone within the convenience of your home to get a good idea of the strength of your vagal tone. You can do this with the help of a friend. It might also be a new and excellent weekend activity for you— more pleasant than the pesky work email that ruined Susan's weekend! Knowing your vagal tone can have a profound impact on your self-awareness.

Vagal Tone Testing

The way to test vagal tone is through your mouth. The vagus nerve runs through your neck, and the ventral vagal aspect of the nerve has a vital role in the workings of the throat. If you can open your mouth comfortably, you can do this little test.

1. Get a helper, like a friend or family member.

2. Get a flashlight. And give your helper the flashlight.

3. Open your mouth wide.

4. Your helper looks in your mouth and focuses on the back at the point where the teardrop uvula dangles in the center of your throat.

5. Slowly vocalize and say *"aaaaah"* a few times.

6. Your helper watches what your uvula does as you say the *"aaaaah"* sound and tells you.

7. If your uvula moves up evenly, consistently, and symmetrically, you have a good functioning ventral vagal nerve. Your social engagement state is on and in good shape.

8. If your uvula moves to one side, there is likely an imbalance in the functioning of this nerve.

Physical, Mental, and Emotional Symptoms

The vagus nerve influences many conditions that affect our physical, mental, and emotional states. It travels from the brain stem, touching and stimulating almost every major body organ except the adrenal glands. This is why it is tied to the functioning of your body's organ systems.

Anxiety and Stress

Heart rate variability is influenced by the vagus nerve's capacity to regulate the body's rhythms. A person's HRV describes the natural ebb and flow of their heart beating in time with their breathing. Greater resilience indicates a higher heart rate variability in the face of adversity and results from a high vagal tone. On the other hand, reduced HRV resulting from a low vagal tone is linked to ongoing stress, anxiety, and emotional dysregulation that continues even after a stressful incident has finished.

Food Intake and Gut Health

The posterior vagal trunk has a very apt name— "hunger nerve." It is a conduit of the more significant vagus nerve operating on the lungs, heart, and gastrointestinal system. When your stomach is empty, the hunger nerve tells your brain you need food. Signals that travel via the vagus nerve from the stomach to the brain have a crucial influence on your moods— hungry, satisfied, overfed, or simply *hangry,* where your hunger reaches a point of no return, and you feel like you will shout at anyone who approaches you until you have eaten. Naturally, these moods influence your stress and inflammatory responses.

Signals run down via the vagus nerve from the brain to the stomach, influencing the release of digestive enzymes and the function of enteroendocrine cells that begin secreting gut hormones to suppress the appetite. These signals also play a role in determining gastrointestinal motility. Said another way, that means where you belong on the scale of constipation to explosive diarrhea and everything in between.

Immunity And Autoimmune Diseases

Every body part is minutely connected, and the vagus nerve coordinates many communication pathways aiding these connections. Signals constantly travel from the brain to the chest and abdomen, as well as from the gut to the central nervous system. The vagus nerve is the conductor of this orchestral performance by telling the brain to release neurotransmitters and hormones, regulating stress, coordinating responses, and keeping inflammation in check.

For instance, it coordinates the parasympathetic response of relaxation, which slows breathing and heart rate, and stimulates digestion which in turn has a soothing effect on inflammation. To coordinate this entire function, it releases a neurotransmitter called acetylcholine which acts as a brake against chronic inflammation.

As time goes on, the impact on autoimmune illnesses from vagus nerve activation may be pretty positive. A vagal inflammatory reflex inhibits the synthesis of cytokines, some of which are involved in autoimmune diseases. *Tumor Necrosis Factor* is the scientific name for these compounds. In healthy individuals, TNF is blocked by the immune system. Still, in people with autoimmune diseases, an excess of TNF enters the circulation, leading to inflammation and worsening symptoms.

Many medications used to treat rheumatoid arthritis aim to reduce levels of TNF. Since drugs that target TNF also inhibit the immune response and have other undesirable side effects, enhancing this naturally occurring reaction in the vagus nerve would have a comparable impact, or possibly a better one since there would be no detrimental side effects.

Blood Pressure and Heart Rate

The heart can become incapable of pumping enough blood throughout the body if the vagus nerve is hyperactive. Cognition loss and organ failure are linked to abnormally high vagal nerve activity. A vagus nerve disorder is one of the most prevalent causes of passing out, called vasovagal syncope. It happens when the vagus nerve is overstimulated when the body overreacts to specific stimuli.

In this situation, both blood pressure and heart rate decrease. Although vasovagal syncope often doesn't need treatment, someone having frequent fainting episodes should see a doctor. If the vagus nerve is hyperactive, the heartbeat may slow to a dangerously low rate (bradycardia). First-degree heart block may also occur in those with meager heart rates due to an overactive vagus nerve.

Mood, Anxiety, and Depression

The vagus nerve is intrinsically tied to managing sadness, fear, and other emotions. Our brain receives information linked to anxiety, fear, and stress via the vagus nerve, leading to an experience many commonly identify as a "gut feeling." When our vagus system is not working at its optimum level, we lose the ability to connect with these intuitive patterns. Therefore, we make more wrong decisions because we cannot trust ourselves.

Your SNS activates the "fight-flight-freeze" response whenever the brain identifies a danger. In contrast, the PSNS serves to relax you. After an immediate threat has passed, the PSNS takes control, such as when a person is rescued from oncoming vehicles while crossing the street. Having been relieved of your anxiety, you may now relax. However, the brain may occasionally stay in a panic state even after the threat has passed. If this happens too often, you may enter a state of prolonged, chronic anxiety and depression because you are constantly anxious and worried about things outside your immediate realm of control.

Consider an orchestra. You need a conductor to carry the rhythm. Without them, there would be very talented musicians, but all would make whatever music and rhythm they wanted. The audience wouldn't hear the cello's lilt or the guitar's strumming. They'd experience noise. When a conductor takes over, they bring *the balance that alters noise to music.*

In the same way, your vagus nerve is your body's conductor. It brings order to the functions of your organs. It helps your guts, heart, and voice produce music, not chaos. It gives a tune-up to otherwise tuned-out emotions. When you turn inward to check with your feelings and connect to your inner expressiveness, you work to stimulate the vagus nerve and give yourself a release from depressing, anxious thoughts.

Digestive Issues

Damage to your vagus nerve can cause gastroparesis, where food does not move in your intestines. In those with gastroparesis, the stomach's muscles cannot move freely, and typically, a condition known as motility impairment. Usually, your digestive system is propelled by powerful muscle contractions. Gastroparesis, on the other hand, causes abnormally slow or nonexistent stomach motility, which prevents the stomach from emptying normally.

Nerve damage to the vagus nerve is the underlying cause of gastroparesis. When functioning normally, the vagus nerve causes the muscles in your stomach to contract or tighten to facilitate food's movement through the digestive system. Lifestyle diseases like diabetes may cause damage to your vagus nerve, which can result in gastroparesis. Because of this, food cannot go from the stomach to the intestines, and you may get abdominal pain. Other complications associated with gastroparesis include:

- Food stays in the stomach too long and runs the risk of fermenting and increasing the chances of harmful gut bacteria growth.

- Hardening the food into a solid mass called bezoars can cause stomach blockages and prevent food from passing to the small intestine.

- Blood sugar levels rise rapidly when the food finally leaves the stomach to enter the small intestine.

- Poor nutrition.

- Dehydration.

<u>Erectile Dysfunction</u>
Perpetual states of worry and tension result from the constant activation of fight-flight-freeze responses. In turn, these states create a chatter in our heads and compel our minds to be on edge. Under normal circumstances, you need to be in a state of arousal to get to and sustain an erection from

a state of relaxation. In other words, you are primed for intercourse in the parasympathetic state. If you are in the fight-flight-freeze state, looking at anything outside the lens of worry and anxiety becomes difficult. Suppose your mind is constantly thinking about information that stresses you. Erectile dysfunction is the byproduct because you are way too stressed to relax.

Imagine trying to engage in something intimate while your internal organs tell you, "There's a thief in the house; run for your life!" You get drawn to the fear, the body is primed for a fight, flight, or freeze— and you lose your erection, leading to dysfunction. These responses happen at a latent level that you may not consciously realize.

Brain Fugue

Have you ever experienced lapses in time when nothing makes sense? You try to focus on the work because you have deadlines that must be taken care of, but no matter what you do, your mind cannot process anything. This is a case of brain fog, where you are disoriented and you cannot narrow your focus and get anything done. Brain fog also indicates that your vagus nerve isn't functioning ideally.

The delicate interaction between your brain and stomach is controlled by the millions of neurons in your central nervous system. These neurons transmit information from your brain to your gastrointestinal system.

Remember how your stomach churns in preparation for an important presentation? Or, think of how your mouth waters at recollecting a meal you like. The emotions you experience are signals sent back and forth between your brain and digestive system. The vagus nerve is the primary nerve responsible for transmitting these signals. Naturally, if it is not operating as it should be, it will affect the optimal performance of your brain.

Brain fog may manifest itself in several ways, including forgetfulness, difficulty concentrating, and a need for stimulants such as caffeine, sugar, or alcohol to make it through the day. Your mind is experiencing confusion that lasts for longer than it should. It's feeling like you're running through a fog— and there's a hand trying to bring you to shelter— but it's always out of reach. Brain fugue is a cluster of symptoms. Having trouble concentrating, forgetting things, and thinking about becoming cloudy are all commonly associated problems. Alterations in mood, such as mild depression, irritability, fatigue, and a lack of vigor, indicate that your vagus nerve has taken a hit.

Thyroid Imbalance

Thyroid glands are primarily activated by the vagus nerve, which are part of the parasympathetic branch of the autonomic nervous system. One study that performed a spectral analysis of heart rate variability found hyperthyroidism to be a state of sympathovagal imbalance associated with a falling vagal modulation of our heart rates.

When the sympathetic and vagal components of the autonomic nervous system (ANS) are overactive or underactive, this is known as a sympathetic-vagal (sympathovagal) imbalance. Symptoms of sympathovagal imbalance include increased activity in the sympathetic nervous system and decreased activity in the parasympathetic nervous system.

COVID-19

When the horror of the pandemic was a living, waking reality, many of us experienced recurrent episodes of brain fog after being struck by the virus. Recent research discerns prolonged symptoms of COVID— joint and muscle pain, changes in menstrual patterns, sleep problems, dizziness, depression, anxiety, irritability, heart palpitations, and breathlessness, among others, indicate poor vagus nerve function.

These long-term symptoms affect about 15% of survivors, meaning that issues that should only last the course of the illness end up remaining with them indefinitely. A 2022 report by the *European Society of Clinical Microbiology and Infectious Diseases* looked at the functioning of the vagus nerve in patients who are still experiencing symptoms post-COVID. They found most long-term subjects reported a range of vagus nerve dysfunctions, inclusive of functional alterations in some cases. Issues included nerves becoming thicker, difficulty swallowing, and impaired breathing.

Lyme Disease

Before discussing the association of the vagus nerve with Lyme Disease, let's look at what this illness entails. Lyme disease is a vector-borne disease that occurs in excessive concentration in some parts of the world, including the United States. It is caused by a bacterium, *Borrelia burgdorferi*, although in rare cases, it can also be the work of *Borrelia mayonii*. In humans, it is most commonly transmitted through the bite of infected back-legged ticks, usually deer ticks.

Typical Lyme disease symptoms include headaches, feverishness, fatigue, and, if lucky, a skin rash. Lucky because if you get this rash, you know you have been infected with Lyme disease. Unlucky if you don't because the symptoms of Lyme are similar to having cold-like symptoms or being run down and it may take longer to diagnose. If untreated, the illness can affect the heart, joints, and nervous system. Lyme disease is notoriously difficult to cure and may have long-lasting effects because the bacterium that causes it is typically challenging to identify. The infection can cause irreversible deterioration of the joints and other tissues in the worst situations.

The connection between the vagus nerve and Lyme Disease is an ongoing research topic. Still, evidence suggests patients with chronic manifestations may get affected by the irritation of the nerve and experience vasovagal syncope, which is fainting caused by the overstimulation of the vagus nerve. The bacteria responsible for causing Lyme disease can enter the ANS and disrupt the vagus nerve's functions.

Additionally, researchers believe cardiac vagal tone can be affected by *borrelia* bacteria. When this happens, one of the essential functions of the vagus nerve— which is to help in heart rate regulation and activity, gets disrupted. The concerning issue is when the vagus nerve gets affected because of Lyme disease, impacted individuals not only deal with the symptoms native to the sickness but also have to contend with other malfunctions associated with a faltering ANS.

Talk with your healthcare provider

Consider pausing and taking a few deep breaths. At this stage, you may think that what was just covered may match a symptom or two or some issues you have faced. Perhaps you are wondering if you can help yourself and experience a life free of health challenges and problems associated with them. Alternatively, maybe you have just felt "something" was out of order.

Or maybe what you are reading here is a road sign pointing you in a more positive, hopeful direction on your journey to better health. Yes, making fundamental changes take time, effort, and commitment. Real change inherently involves many, many small steps of change. It is possible to make small changes in the comfort of your own home, to work toward feeling healthier, happier, and more peaceful.

Reach out to your friends and family, medical professionals, and healthcare providers about your symptoms and what you are experiencing to get the help you need. Go for your annual checkup and follow-up appointments, and make an appointment with your chosen healthcare provider for anything you are concerned about. Share that you want to include support for your vagus nerve's health. Talk to them about testing your vagus nerve in their office and what you found out with your at-home test. What steps would they recommend? Working collaboratively, you advocate for your health, they share their expertise, and together you can come to a consensus about possible next steps. On the journey towards improved health, getting more precise and transparent about what you can do to improve your health is a good idea. So, before making any health-related changes, speak with your medical professional and healthcare provider. They are there to be a part of your journey.

Part 1 is now complete. This means the science bit is over. In the next chapter, we will look at ways to stimulate and strengthen this wandering nerve.

My Reflections & Notes

Use this section to review your healthcare team. Which ones do you currently have? Which ones have you been meaning to get? Do you feel comfortable with the healthcare providers you have? What are the priority appointments that you need to make? Once you reach out to them, you can begin your journey into implementing these natural, non-invasive methods to live life lit by the magic of a well-functioning vagus nerve.

My current healthcare team is:

Other health Providers I feel could really help me are:

What changes do I need to make to my healthcare team so it is a better fit between my health provider and me?

What appointments do I know I need to make?

Other helpful ideas and notes:

Part Two

Restoring Ease and Renewing Your Mind-Body Connection

The Methods

*"**W**E NEED TO GET the body into states in which it can regulate and feel more comfortable with itself."* ~ Stephen Porges, Ph.D.

Chapter 4

Calming Your Mind
The Methods

THIS CHAPTER COVERS NATURAL methods to support the vagus nerve through exercises that calm the mind. Using them regularly may help you address the impact of short- and long-term stressors at home. It's impossible to be the best version of yourself for the people you love and this world without being that for yourself.

Here's a cliche: "the most productive thing you can do sometimes is just to do nothing." In this contemporary age, we can get so caught up in our hectic lifestyles and exhausting deadlines that we often push the need to calm down to the background when "the time permits." Before we know it, we work ten to twelve or more hours daily, five, six, or seven days a week.

In the journey of regaining our health, methods that support the healing and wellness of the vagus nerve and the nervous system are generally exercises that make us slow down. They are resting moments for our body, mind, heart, and spirit. Rest days are essential. Athletes will emphasize that there are days when taking a break is needed. This is a time to let loose and relax. This effectively gives the body time to rest and recuperate so overall performance isn't diminished by too much strain and stress.

As a friendly reminder, not all stress is bad, and way too much stress is. A certain amount helps us cope with difficult situations that can spring up in our daily lives. Physical responses return to normal when the problem is gone, and we return to everyday life. On the other hand, there's a negative impact when we don't bounce back from being stressed. Prolonged stress can affect our mental, physical, and emotional well-being. It changes how we react to people and situations. In addition, prolonged stress can change our body's way of behaving. Overwhelming stress may manifest in various physical forms, including headaches, strain in the shoulders and neck, dizziness, exhaustion, and disturbed sleep. This is because the stress hormone cortisol disrupts regular brain activity, contributing to the harmful effects of stress on our overall health, especially our physical, mental, and emotional health. This contributes to anxiety, inability to focus, indecision, and other adverse cognitive outcomes. Emotional manifestations include but are not limited to impatience, feelings of being overburdened, anxiety, poor self-esteem, and sadness. Extreme stress may lead to hostile or defensive behavior, social isolation, difficulty communicating, overconsumption of alcohol and tobacco, and other adverse activities. In the long run, there's only so much your body can tolerate before it cries out for help.

Being a better you and helping your health begins with calming down. An excellent place to start is with our thinking minds and using our physical bodies to help. Calming the mind is a challenge with most states of mind. Even someone feeling good can find it hard to stop and focus solely on one thing, like breathing. Practicing and remembering how to focus takes time and dedication. And to get there takes patience for yourself.

Are you willing? If you want to explore this, you'll be working towards changing into healthier habits that help your health. Hopefully, experiencing the benefits in your whole body and being, feeling space open up in your heart and mind, and noticing less tension or distress in your body will motivate you to continue.

Tips for success for all methods:

- Have a timer.

- Before any of the following exercises, ensure you have enough time to complete them without feeling rushed or pressured. This includes being patient with yourself.

- Create a comfortable space in your home. It can be any nook or corner of your home. You can also designate a place for doing your breathing exercises in your home. This could be your front porch, the bed, the living room floor, the garden, or a comfortable chair on your patio. It can also be in your office with your chair facing a window to the sky or a tree or a concrete wall.

- Create a distraction-free environment for as long as you practice the exercises. This includes preventing interruptions, silencing your devices (or turning them off), putting up a sign, etc.

- Be in an upright position that is comfortable for you, your back, and your body.

- Start with two minutes of practicing, then build on it over time. Work towards ten minutes or more. Start with once a day and work up to three times each day.

- Breathe in and out your nose, ideally. Or breathe in through your nose and out your mouth if that is more comfortable for you. If it isn't, then breathe in whatever way feels good.

- The goal is to create a routine ingrained in your muscle memory, like brushing your teeth and sipping your morning cuppa of sunshine.

The Power of Deep Breathing

In recent years, notable studies have observed that longer exhalations improve heart rate variability and help the vagus nerve recover so that we are not stuck in a perpetual state of fight-flight-freeze. Heart rate variability is the healthy fluctuation in the intervals between heartbeats. All living animals have this.

The breathing cycle has an inhalation and an exhalation phase. On inhaling, the SNS (sympathetic nervous system) causes a brief heart rate acceleration. On exhaling, the vagus nerve secretes a substance called Ach that helps send signals from one nerve cell to the next, causing the heartbeat to slow down and consequently activating the PSNS (parasympathetic nervous system) and enabling the rest-and-digest system into action.

Slower breathing, with an added focus on those longer exhalations, can stimulate the vagus nerve and help achieve a strong HRV, according to a review of studies. Your heart rate variability is a part of the fitness of your vagus nerve, its vagal tone, and the way it responds. A higher HRV is a sign of solid vagus nerve health, which means lower stress, better cognition, and an overall healthy state. Therefore, strengthening your heart rate variability is an excellent way to improve your vagal tone, combat undue stress, and help an overactive nervous system driven by a fight, flight or freeze response.

Breathing techniques to calm and focus the mind are as ancient as civilizations. These techniques resurface from diverse cultures in the modern day through practices like Yoga and Tai Chi. These practices regularly embrace slow, meditative breathing patterns. They concentrate on moderating how we breathe by gently shifting the breathing to longer exhalations (compared to inhalations), enabling practitioners to identify their natural breathing consciously. Breathing this way moves awareness to focus on the act of respiration as beginning with the abdomen instead of the upper chest and head. In other words, when you breathe with awareness, you ensure your in-breaths are happening from the stomach, not the nose or chest.

The vagus nerve loves when you breathe well. Breathing well is a simple yet powerful way to tell your body and your vagus nerve that you are okay right now. It's an effective way to bring more oxygen into your body, help your nerve wake up, and notice that there is no real threat so that it can move from the fight-flight-freeze mode of operation to the rest-and-digest mode. Breathing correctly literally tells your vagus nerve, "It's okay. We're okay." There's a phrase for this. It's called "respiratory biofeedback." This is your body's built-in method of biofeedback. Breathing enhances the balance of physical, mental, and emotional health, which helps with managing stress and performance. Breathing well is a love letter to your vagus nerve.

Before you begin, let's explore whether or not you are breathing properly:

Breath Check-In

Are you breathing well? Many people don't breathe well and often breathe using only their upper chest area. Would you like to take a moment and discover if you are? This checking in with your breathing can be done at any time. This will help you really see if you are breathing fully or shallowly.

1. Transition into stopping whatever you are doing and continue to breathe the same way, without changing your breathing pattern.

2. Put one hand on your chest.

CALMING YOUR MIND

3. Put the other hand on your belly.

4. Look at your hands. Notice how your hands are moving.

5. Ask yourself: "Is the hand on my belly moving in and out more while the hand on my chest moves slightly? Or is the hand on my belly moving slightly while the hand on my chest is moving in and out more?"

6. Continue to breathe for a few more seconds to confirm your sense of how your hands are moving.

Here's what it means. When the hand on your belly moves in and out more noticeably, and the other hand on your chest moves slightly, you are breathing calmly and relaxedly. When the hand on your belly is moving slightly, and the hand on your chest is moving in and out more noticeably, you are breathing shallowly which indicates that you are not breathing well and are likely experiencing stress.

Diaphragmatic Breathing

Diaphragmatic Breathing is a breathing method that encourages the full use of your lungs. When you bring life-enhancing air into your lungs, you send a quietly strong message to your body that all is well right now. Practicing this exercise over time encourages you to shift from shallow breathing to a more natural breath. There are two positions you can experience diaphragmatic breathing in. Either you are sitting up or lying belly down.

<u>Diaphragmatic Breathing Sitting Up Method</u>

1. Set your timer for two minutes (or more when you're ready).

2. Take a moment and find a comfortable position.

3. Begin by taking a few deep, slow full breaths. As you do,

4. Slowly breathe in, in, in, and follow your breath into your belly.

5. As you breathe in feel your belly move gently out. Gently feel your lungs filling up from the bottom of your lungs to the top and take in the air fully.

6. When your inhale is done, begin to exhale out, out, out.

7. As you exhale, feel your shoulders soften and drop while your belly relaxes.

8. Repeat steps 3 through 6

<u>Diaphragmatic Breathing Belly Down Method</u>

This is a very simple way to experience breathing fully using diaphragmatic breathing only if your body can be comfortable lying belly down and fully on the floor or bed. Trying this out a few times is a good way to get your muscle memory going so you can more easily do this breathing method in the sitting or standing position. If you are able to be in this position safely, easily, and comfortably then:

1. Fold your arms on the floor at the level of your head and place your forehead on your forearms. Your legs are unbent and spread about once to twice the width of your head.

2. Once you are comfortable, simply breathe.

3. Take a few moments and what do you notice about your breathing? In this position, you automatically breathe using your diaphragm. Notice how your belly moves and your chest moves only slightly.

When you are ready:

1. Begin to slowly breathe in, in, in, and follow your breath into your belly.

2. As you breathe in feel your belly move gently out. Gently feel your lungs filling up from the bottom of your lungs to the top and take in the air fully.

3. When your inhale is done, begin to exhale out, out, out.

4. Do this a few times.

Next steps after breathing properly

Now that you know how to breathe properly, let's move on and explore other breathing methods that help your vagus nerve in about 2 minutes. Yes, two minutes. Two minutes to shift into rest and digest mode using an appropriate breathing technique with a longer exhalation. A 2019 study shares that a mere two minutes of deep breathing can work wonders. The researchers opine that this can engage the vagus nerve, improve cognition, and increase HRV. So, whenever a decision feels too complex or challenging, or you don't know what to do next, breathing for two minutes can be the difference between getting overwhelmed and making a better choice.

How do you do this? You don't need expensive gadgets or devices to show you the way. To keep it simple, you need to permit yourself to take a break, have a physical place to practice, and have a timer. Typically, most of us associate deep breathing with meditating while sitting on a pillow in a crossed-legged position, but that will only work if you are comfortable. Instead, choose a way to sit in a seated posture that makes your back erect in a relaxed way, with your stomach free from constrictions, so that you can make the most of these natural methods.

4:8 Deep Breath

The 4:8 Deep Breath is one of the most uncomplicated and potent ways to reorient your vagus nerve for better health. It provides the benefits that the longer exhale gives our bodies. In this method, inhaling for four counts and exhaling for eight will complete one breathing cycle. So your out-breath is twice as long as your in-breath. And a "count" doesn't need to mean a "second" of time. A count is your rhythmic timing. Use this exercise the next time you feel like the stress around and within you is becoming overwhelming. Or better yet, use it regularly to manage stress and help you not become overwhelmed.

4:8 Deep Breath Method

1. Set your timer for two minutes (or more when you're ready).

2. Inhaling, take a deep diaphragmatic breath through your stomach *via* your nostrils. Your belly should expand, then as you fill up, it will constrict until you can't take in any more air. This is your count of four.

3. Exhaling slowly through pursed, narrow opening of your lips, just like you are blowing out candles on a cake to the count of eight.

4. Repeat steps 2 and 3 until the timer goes off.

Breath Focusing

You can implement Breath Focusing in all your exercises, including the 4:8 Deep Breathing practice. This means using a mental picture or repeating a meaningful word or phrase that helps to focus your attention. For example, choose a simple, calming, peaceful image, like a candle, the wind blowing through a tree, a star, the moon, or the blue sky. You can also choose a meaningful one or 2-syllable word or a concise phrase that reinforces a state of stillness or calm. For example, "Thank you," "Amen," "Peace," "Renew," "In. Out," "Stillness," or another meaningful word to you.

<u>Breath Focusing with a mental picture method</u>

1. Set your timer for two minutes (or more when you're ready).

2. As you breathe in, imagine that the air is a source of vibrant, beautiful energy that gives you the ability to be a better you. Remember when inhaling to take a deep breath, diaphragmatically, through your stomach *via* your nostrils. Your abdomen should expand, then as you fill up, it will constrict until you can't take in any more air. Visualizing at the same time that you are filling up your lungs and body with vibrant, life-giving air, and it's washing through your body. This is your count of four.

3. As you breathe out, to the count of eight through the pursed, narrow opening of your lips, visualize the air carrying away any built-up distress and tension on the winds of your out-breath.

4. Repeat until the timer goes off.

<u>Breath Focusing with a meaningful word or phrase method</u>

1. Choose a word or phrase.

2. Set your timer for two minutes (or more when you're ready).

3. As you breathe in, silently say the first syllable of your word, phrase, or 1-syllable word. (Remember when inhaling to take a deep breath, diaphragmatically, through your stomach *via* your nostrils. Your abdomen should expand, then as you fill up, it will constrict until you can't take in any more air. This is your count of four.)

4. As you breathe out, silently say the second syllable or 1-syllable word. (Remember, it's through the pursed, narrow opening of your lips to the count of eight).

5. Repeat until the timer goes off.

Equal-Timed Breaths

With this method, your inhales and exhales are equal. This is a great way to gently exercise your breathing muscles and encourage deeper breaths. Start with a count of five for breathing in, then a count of five for breathing out. After practice, move to six, seven, eight counts, and so on. Build up your strength at your own pace. Take it slowly.

1. Set your timer for two minutes (or more when you're ready).

2. As you breathe in and inhale to the count of five through your stomach via your nostrils, your abdomen expands as you fill up, then it begins to contract until you can't take any more air in for your full inhale.

3. As you breathe out to the count of five with a pursed, narrow opening of your lips, your chest and belly soften as you fully exhale.

4. Repeat until the timer goes off.

Progressive Muscle Relaxation

This method involves taking deep breaths while tightening a specific muscle group and releasing them, which helps you feel what relaxing feels like. When doing this, use any deep breathing method above. For the directions,

CALMING YOUR MIND

the Equal-Time Breaths Method will be used. Set aside 20 minutes to do this.

- Set your timer for 20 minutes (or more when you're ready).

- Begin with a few deep breaths.

- Once you feel ready, breathe in and simultaneously tense the feet muscles. Do this for four counts.

- Breathe out, soften your feet muscles and release the held tension in the feet. Do this for four counts.

- Breathe in and simultaneously tense your calf muscles for four counts.

- Breathe out and release stored tension in the calves for four counts.

- Continue to slowly work your way up each muscle group as you follow the same pattern of breathing in and tensing a muscle group to the count of four, breathing out, and releasing the tension to four.

- Continue with your thighs, abdomen, chest, fingers, arms, shoulders, neck, and face.

Lion's Breath

This method involves taking a deep breath and exhaling like a lion yawning. Open your mouth as big as is comfortable on the out-breath.

- Set your timer for two minutes (or more when you're ready).

- Begin with a few deep breaths.

- Breathe in through your nose until your belly feels full of air and you cannot take in any more.

- Open your mouth as big as you can comfortably.

- Breathe out slowly and loudly with a "Haaaaaa" sound.

- Experience the air leaving your body and taking the tension and troubles of the day away.

- Repeat as many times as you like.

Walking Meditation

The breathing methods discussed have been in a sitting position, but did you know you can also do breathing exercises while walking? This is different from suggesting or recommending that you practice this method to cross a busy road. There are ways to do this to reap benefits and also be safe. The idea behind this is to focus on your steps, your footing, and how you are walking. Using your breath helps you get in and observe how you move. You meditate on your walking.

To prepare yourself, you'll need to do a few things. First, choose a location to walk and decide how many minutes you'll take. The recommendation is to start with ten minutes and increase as you feel ready. In choosing a location, get creative. If you live in a crowded urban space, find a place inside or outside that is safe where you feel at ease to walk. For example, if your apartment has a roof terrace, choose a time to visit when it is quiet. Alternatively, find a safe walkway, like a lane, hallway, or stairs, on which you can walk back and forth. The main thing here is that the spot should be quieter and not noisy, and it should feel safe, comfortable, and easy to be there. There's no need to worry about the distance you'll cover because you are not trying to reach a destination or burn calories. Instead, you are practicing a very intentional form of attuning your mind to how your physical body moves, using your breath to help.

Deliberate steps are the hallmark of meditative walking. The most critical aspect is that it is the natural way you walk. It's not a fake or contrived way of walking. This includes your hands, too. No matter what seems most natural to you, whether it is clasping your palms behind your back, directly in front, or letting them dangle at your side, allow it. Lastly, start with small steps until you get used to this method.

Give each step careful consideration that they deserve. Reflect on each action. It may seem strange, even silly, or just new and different. There will be moments when your mind may wander during this, too. This is entirely normal, and you don't need to feel guilty or think you have missed out on the benefits of this. This takes practice. The more time you give to it, the easier the process becomes of your mind settling into your body's walking patterns as a meditative, calming experience. The end goal is to help you experience slowing down so your vagus nerve can turn on that PSNS's rest and digest mode, to help you restore your health.

There are seven main walking parts to remember as you explore this Walking Meditation. Feel free to adjust this general overview to meet the comfort and safety of how your body walks.

1. Lift one foot.

2. Moving the foot, you lift forward from where you stand.

3. Place the foot down on the floor from the heel first, then the front, and finally the toes.

4. Shift the weight of your body to the front leg of the foot you just moved forward while you lift the heel of the back foot, ensuring your toes remain in contact with the ground.

5. Lift the back foot entirely off the ground.

6. Observing the back foot swing forward and lower as the heel first makes contact with the ground.

7. Feel the weight of your body shift onto that foot and notice the experience of moving forward.

8. Repeat steps 1 to 7.

The method of putting the Walking Meditation into motion:
- Stand relaxed at the starting point.
- Take a few deep breaths using any method you like.
- Begin to walk along the path you have chosen.
- *Pay close attention as you walk to a sensation you might ordinarily ignore, such as any change in your breathing or how your legs synchronize with your feet to help you move.

*Consciously notice the weight of your head resting on your neck and shoulders, the sounds around you, the motions in your body propelling you forward, and the sights and sounds that come into focus before your eyes. The smells of your environment.
- Return to taking a few deep breaths using any method you like.
- Continue to walk along your chosen path and repeat the steps with the asterisks (*) until your time is up.

Mindfulness Meditation For Your Vagus Nerve

There is a lot of exciting, life-changing research about the benefits of mindfulness meditation in stimulating the vagus nerve. One such paper found that it brings down the severity of depression. Another discovered mindfulness meditation could be essential in lowering chronic inflammation and enhancing the brain's stress and anxiety management capabilities.

In particular, the second study, conducted by researchers from Carnegie Mellon University, identified mindful meditation as a way to improve resilience to stress and enhance the function of the vagus nerve. The subjects of the study were thirty-five job-seeking adults who were facing the pressures of unemployment. They participated in a three-day mindfulness meditation or a relaxation retreat without a mindfulness component. The adults who underwent mindfulness meditation training witnessed a lowering of inflammation levels while enhancing cognitive function. Those who participated in the retreat without mindfulness meditation relaxed but did not experience these additional benefits. This and other studies speak to mindfulness meditation engaging the body to naturally self-heal.

Additionally, according to studies, mindfulness meditation reduces activity associated with the aspect of our brain responsible for those wakeful restful states that can be experienced throughout the day. Sometimes, too much time is spent this way: daydreaming, idle thinking, reflective self-thoughts, or a wandering mind. It's when a person's mind is not actively engaged with the external environment. Mindfully meditating is an active process that encourages focusing on what's happening right now, wherever you are. In doing so, the wandering mind returns to the present moment, and the vagus nerve is positively impacted by getting the message that all is well in the environment. Mindfulness meditation is a non-invasive natural method that calms the mind and restores the body.

The steps of a mindfulness meditation practice are simple, and at the same time, actually doing it can be challenging. When you begin, the activities may even be irritating because they require a commitment of time every day, and your daily habits get interrupted. However, if the information shared here motivates you, follow it and take the step to start. Mindfully meditating can feel like and be a safe space where you have moments of slowing down and restoring ease. It is a small and powerful way to relieve stress and retreat from the daily noise surrounding you. It's a way to focus on you and your beautiful being and renew your mind-body connection.

Basic Mindfulness Meditation

Mindful meditation develops awareness of being mindful throughout daily life so that every moment spent awake is conscious, deliberate, and intentional. Honestly, it is not easy. There will be plenty of moments when the mind will wander because that's what it's wired to do. It is not about emptying your mind; instead, it brings the mind back when it wanders with a simple message: "Let's focus on this present right now."

A few tips when you practice: Your mind will roam. This is normal. You will notice different things happening around you— perhaps a "ting" from your phone that reminds you there's a deadline due soon or your favorite show will start in a bit. You could get lost in thoughts and begin daydreaming about things that have happened, or that may come in your life. Or you may remember a bit of gossip you read about a celebrity, notice thoughts about them and start judging. This is all normal. *There is nothing wrong with any of it.* Thinking is to your mind what breathing is to your nose. It's natural. Lastly, if you are tired and not well-rested, you may feel drowsy at the onset or even be tempted to fall asleep. If you do fall asleep, that's okay.

Mindfulness meditation interrupts our unconsciousness awareness of our roaming mind thinking about things in the future or the past to help bring conscious awareness to what's happening in the present moment by refocusing attention with gentleness to the breath. Every time the mind wanders, notice it, and label it "Thought" or "Thinking" For example, if you notice you're thinking about "My shopping list." Notice the thought, mark it as "Thought," then take a moment and inhale deeply. And gently return your attention to your breath. In this way, you gently let go of what you were thinking about and refocus your attention on your breathing instead of the thought. Focusing on your breath puts you in the present moment. Whenever the mind wanders, acknowledge what you were thinking about and don't judge yourself or think, "I've failed." Instead, take a moment, refocus on your breath, and continue.

Mindful Meditation with Breath as the Focus Method

1. Set your timer for two minutes (or more when ready)

2. Take a few deep breaths of the 4:8 Breathing Technique or another favorite.

3. Continue to focus on your breathing.

4. Notice when you're mind wanders and label it as a "Thought."

5. Return to focus on your breathing.

6. Repeat until the timer goes off.

Mindful Meditation with Counting Breaths as the Focus

1. Set your timer for two minutes (or more when ready).

2. Take a few deep breaths of the 4:8 Breathing Technique or another favorite.

3. Continue to focus on your breathing.

4. Count each in and out breath until your focus organically returns to the present.

5. Notice when you're mind wanders and label it as a "Thought."

6. Return to focus on counting your breathing.

7. Repeat until the timer goes off.

Yoga

There are more than a few styles of Yoga. For our purposes, we are referring to gentle Yoga—styles like Hatha, Yin, Restorative Yoga, and Yoga Nidra. Gentle Yoga is a natural and non-invasive way to stimulate the vagus nerve. The benefit of Yoga is well-researched and uses breathing and movement exercises that induce an overall state of balance. You aim to reach a stage where you can exist as a relaxed but waking human. Let's focus on one seated yoga stretch that helps balance the vagus nerve through the gentle twisting movement of the throat, chest, belly, and spine.

Seated Yoga Stretch

- Sit on a comfortable chair with your feet planted firmly on the ground, uncrossed.

- Place your left hand outside your right leg.

- Place your right hand behind you on the back of a chair or your lower back.

- Inhale and lengthen your spine.

- Hold for two counts.

- Exhale and gently twist your upper body to the right.

- Take several breaths in and out, visualizing your digestive organs getting massaged by your breathing.

- Slowly untwist your upper body and return to the center.

- Pause and take a few more breaths. Once you feel ready, switch sides and repeat the exercise to the left.

- Slowly untwist your upper body and return to the center.

- Take note of your experience— mental, physical, emotional, and spiritual.

Yoga Nidra

A form of meditation, often referred to as *yogic sleep,* Yoga Nidra is practiced lying down. This form of Yoga aims to draw your attention to your inner state to bring you to a place where you are balanced between wakefulness and sleep. As a result, your body returns to its natural state, where everything is guided by equilibrium, otherwise known as homeostasis. As a result, your breathing becomes balanced and quiet, your attention becomes mindful, and you become aware of being fully present.

Here are a few tips. First, since you will be lying down with your face up, choose a comfortable spot on your back where you'll be undisturbed. If you like, use a blanket, so you don't get chilled. Make lying on your back feel good and relaxed for you. Ensure you have enough time. Thirty minutes is the average time this takes, but once you learn it, you can do it in a shorter amount of time. You will be bringing awareness to body parts. You can, if you want, mentally say statements like "I am now aware of my right foot." "I am noticing my right knee relax." "Now, my thigh is joining the right knee and becoming relaxed." "I have now relaxed my right hip." "My entire right leg is completely and consciously relaxed." Use what words feel right for you. Lastly, the final step is resting for a couple of minutes is part of the process. This will make your breath flow through the left nostril and cool your body.

Yoga Nidra Basic Steps

1. Lie down on your back. Be very comfortable.

2. Close your eyes and use the 4:8 Breathing Technique. Be slow, relaxed, and easy with your breathing.

CALMING YOUR MIND

3. Bring your mind's attention to your right foot. Notice your foot. Keep the mind there for a few seconds. Use your breath. Consciously relax the muscles in the right foot.

4. After a few seconds, slowly move your attention to your shin and right knee. Notice them. Keep the mind there for a few seconds. Use your breath, and consciously relax your shin and right knee muscles.

5. After a few seconds, slowly move your attention to your right thigh and hip. Notice them. Keep the mind there for a few seconds. Use your breath. Consciously relax the muscles in your thigh and knee.

6. Repeat this process for your left leg.

7. Then continue to repeat the process to all parts of the body. Use your breathing and consciously allow your mind to relax your buttocks, pelvis, stomach, buttocks, lower back, navel region, chest, shoulders, upper back, arms, wrists, hands, palms, and fingers. Your neck and face to the top of your head.

8. Once you reach the top of your head, take a few deep breaths.

9. Notice all the sensations in your body. Is your stomach rumbling? Is there a strand of hair tickling the face? Does the left toe twinge a little? Don't touch anything; breathe and make these observations while relaxing.

10. Slowly turn to the right side and adjust your body so it's curled like when you sit in a chair so it can lie comfortably. Please put your hands under your head to support it.

11. Rest for two minutes or more if you like.

12. In your own time, slowly sit up and open your eyes.

13. Take note of your experience— mental, physical, emotional, and spiritual.

Gentle, Quick Ways to Stimulate the Vagus Nerve

There will be times when stress and anxiety are so overwhelming you can feel yourself spiraling out of control. During such situations, you want a technique that will jolt the vagal nerve into a state of activity, so it can convince your mind that it is okay to calm down and begin relaxing. Here are three techniques that can snap you back quickly but gently.

Deep Breathing

Deep breathing is one of the fastest ways to help your vagus nerve reconnect and help your body and mind. Use any of the techniques described earlier.

Cold water

Exposing the body to a sudden burst of cold, like taking a cold shower or splashing cool water on your face to stimulate the vagus nerve, is simple and effective. As the body adjusts to the sudden decline in temperature, sympathetic activity begins falling, and your PSNS becomes active, setting the resting phase into motion.

Three Buttons

Think of someone close to you— anyone you feel safe around. What do they look like? How are their facial expressions, their voice, or the sense of their touch? Imagine they have a sticker on their forehead that looks like a button with "A" written on it. Next, another sticker on their chin is labeled "B." Then, there's a third sticker with "C" on their wrist.

Imagine you are overwhelmed by something. The minute this happens, stretch out your hand as if you are about to press the "A" button. You see their face, their kind smile, and how their eyes light up when they speak to you. Next, in your mind, press "B." You can now hear their honey-like voice, how soft and soothing it is to your ears. Finally, imagine you are pressing "C." They are now extending their open hand to you so that you can know you are safe. That is all you need to do. Now, your PSNS is active and reigns over your autonomic nervous system. You will slowly begin to calm down, and your mind will return to the present and a more balanced state of function.

Other Tiny Pearls

There are more than a few methods in this book. The abundance of choices might make you reluctant to give any of them a fair shot. Let's bring Susan back for a minute. She's lovely and tends to be worried and nervous, perhaps anxious. So, let's say she gets presented with an entire booklet of different exercises. She's all set to try them out. A friend asks to join in, and they become meditation buddies. Now, on the first attempt, the friend experiences peace and tranquility. Meditation works for her.

Susan, on the other hand, gets annoyed. She feels her hands itching, notices how a tendril of hair keeps flicking her nose, and worries about a million tiny things. At the end of the session, her friend began telling her how wonderful it was. Susan gets deflated, but she decides to fib and says, "Yeah, it worked for me too!" Later on, she calls her friend from home. "Hey, I'm just so caught up with life right now. You carry on with the activities. Maybe I will join a week later." The week becomes a month, then a year. Susan doesn't even try the other activities because she's made up her mind that she's not good at them and broadly thinks, *"They don't work for me"* because of her one-time attempt. It sounds like Susan's making up the last page of her life's story without writing the first page. Have you ever been this way, too?

Feeling better, healing, and improving our health is a series of little steps that have huge effects over time. Before deciding which method is best for you, put each through its paces. These methods are primarily short, need no tech or gear, and can be done almost anywhere. The benefits of most of them can begin to be experienced within a few weeks with regular daily practice. To improve the long-term benefits for life, research shares that it can take 2 – 4 months of consistent daily practice before the benefits are fully realized. And being consistent at the beginning with a daily routine is especially important so you can experience some results and be motivated to continue. Lastly, keeping track of how you feel after feeling these various stress-relieving methods is helpful. Practice daily 3 -4 times a day for 2 minutes. Take note before and after you do a technique each time you practice. Take note of how your body, mind, and heart feel.

My Reflections & Notes

Which methods interested me? For what reason(s) did it pique my interest?

I tried out these methods, and this is what I experienced:

Chapter 5

Biofeedback

"Stress is inner biofeedback ...

"STRESS IS INNER BIOFEEDBACK, signaling you that frequencies are fighting within your system. The purpose of stress isn't to hurt you but to let you know it's time to go back to the heart and start loving."
Sara Paddison

What is Biofeedback?

The methods outlined in this book are all forms of natural biofeedback. Stress is a form of internal biofeedback. For example, Susan notices distress in her body because her pocket pen is sticking into her thigh. Her body signals that distress. She wakes up and witnesses, "Oh, there's pressure on my thigh that shouldn't be there. It's uncomfortable." She looks down and sees her pen. She removes or adjusts the pen. The discomfort goes away. Her body is using its intuitive way of telling her there is distress; her conscious mind wakes up, she can do something, and she has control over her pain, so she removes the pen to lessen discomfort.

Biofeedback equipment uses technology replicating this natural process to help bring awareness so we can respond better. It is a holistic, non-invasive method that trains the senses, the body, and the brain to become better at recognizing a distressed state and returning to a more relaxed, comfortable state. It is natural, too, because the equipment reads your body's responses or brain frequencies and tells you so you can become more aware of them. Finally, it's a way to retrain yourself, especially if you've experienced long-term stress or physical or mental health problems. In many cases, your brain and nervous system relearn how to balance naturally, and with enough training and instruction, biofeedback tools are no longer needed.

The core idea behind biofeedback is to harness your mind's attention and consciously become aware of what is happening in your body. A biofeedback session involves using equipment by a trained professional to collect data on your physiological state and performance. The practitioner will help you move more positively towards achieving your goals based on the data gathered by the devices. Your mental, emotional and physical well-being may benefit from this mind-body treatment. In addition, your health will be under *your* control when you learn to do this.

How Can It Help?

Let's let the research speak for itself. A Task Force of the Society for Neuronal Regulation and the Association for Applied Psychophysiology and Biofeedback outlines criteria for how successful biofeedback interventions are based on evidence from clinical research. The range is from Level One to Level Five. Level Five has the most research available that demonstrates the successful use of biofeedback.

1. Biofeedback level one efficacy is potentially effective in managing eating disorders, improving immune function, aiding recovery from spinal cord injuries, and preventing fainting (syncope).

2. Biofeedback level two efficacy is potentially effective and promising for asthma, autism, cerebral palsy, chronic obstructive pul-

monary disease, bell's palsy, stroke, tinnitus, urinary incontinence in children, post-traumatic stress disorder, erectile dysfunction, depressive disorders, cystic fibrosis, chronic fatigue syndrome, hand dystonia, and irritable bowel syndrome.

3. Biofeedback level three efficacy is potentially helpful for substance abuse and alcohol addiction, diabetes mellitus, fecal incontinence, arthritis, headache, insomnia, traumatic brain injury, urinary incontinence in males, and vulvar vestibulitis.

4. Biofeedback level four efficacy has promising results for anxiety, chronic pain, attention-deficit hyperactivity disorder, epilepsy, constipation in adults, headache in adults, hypertension, motion sickness, Raynaud's disease, and Temporomandibular illness.

5. Biofeedback level Five efficacy is effective for female urinary incontinence.

How It works

There are different types of biofeedback. Most involve electrodes. A licensed professional attaches electrode(s) to your skin in each biofeedback session. These electrodes communicate signals to a monitor, showing an image, emitting a sound, or emanating a light flash evocative of your breathing, heart rate, skin temperature, blood pressure, and muscle activity, depending on the type of biofeedback.

If you are stressed, the patterns of these functions change. For example, the heart rate rises, muscles tighten, blood pressure rises, you sweat profusely, and your breathing increases. These responses show up on the monitor. You get immediate feedback about how your body responds then you learn how to react to them consciously. Biofeedback sessions usually occur in the therapist's office and under supervision.

The biofeedback professional will help you with relevant relaxation exercises to fine-tune different body functions. For instance, they may show you a relaxation technique to turn down those brainwaves that become active when you experience a headache. The technology brings your awareness to unconscious bodily processes more quickly, and practicing exercises to help train your attention and brain are used as well. These include the core methods in this book, like deep breathing, progressive muscle relaxation, mindfulness meditation, and further incorporating calming methods like guided imagery.

Types Of Biofeedback & Practitioners

There are different types of biofeedback depending on your health issues and health goals. Let's take a glance at the different types.

- Brain wave biofeedback: This kind uses scalp sensors and an electroencephalograph to track your brain waves. This is called EEG Biofeedback, Neurofeedback, or Brain Biofeedback.

- Heart Rate biofeedback: This tracks the user's heart rate.

- Breathing biofeedback: Bands are wrapped over the client's stomach and chest to track their breathing and heart rate during respiratory biofeedback.

- Muscle contraction biofeedback: An electromyograph (EMG) sensor is placed on the person's skeletal muscles to record the nerve impulses that trigger muscle contractions.

- Temperature biofeedback: Blood pressure and skin temperature may be tracked using sensors on your fingers and toes. Given that your body temperature decreases in response to stress, seeing that it is abnormally low may motivate you to try some methods for relieving that stress.

- Sweat glands biofeedback An electrodermograph (EDG) is a device that uses sensors to detect the quantity of perspiration on the skin and the activity of the sweat glands, both of which are stress indicators.

Biofeedback requires specialized training in the technology that reads the body's responses to stress. Licensed professionals like psychologists, therapists, counselors, nurses, physiotherapists, physician's assistants, dentists, physical therapists, medical doctors, and researchers are just a few of the many professions that use biofeedback in their careers. It is a powerful ally on the journey to better health. Biofeedback can support the nervous system, help stimulate and support the vagus nerve and relieve distress and suffering for specific health conditions. It is another way to reconnect to your body in a more tangible form that is natural and non-invasive.

My Reflections & Notes

What are my thoughts and feelings about biofeedback?

Chapter 6

Calming Your Body

The Methods

THIS CHAPTER COVERS NATURAL methods to support the vagus nerve through exercises that calm the body. Again, using them regularly may help you address your stress. The body is home to multiple tiny opportunities to learn how to improve our overall health and well-being. Consider for one second how many opportunities this gives us to work with the vagus nerve and support healing in ourselves!

Now, take a minute to think about something you are good at. It could be anything— cooking, cleaning, reading, singing, writing, parenting, finding unique places to visit, fixing things, acing exams— anything. Did you identify it? Good. Picture yourself doing this in two states of mind. In the first state, you are calm, relaxed, and determined. You feel you have your resources in place and are poised to do a good job because your mind is focused and balanced. In the next state, you are anxious for some reason. Your mind is on a million different things. Try as you might you can't narrow your focus to the one thing at hand. The mere thought of it is giving you pins and needles from anxiety. Which state will yield better results? We do better when we feel *safe*. When your vagus nerve is calm, your entire performance will benefit. If it isn't, no matter what you try to do, the results will fall short of what you can achieve.

Sing Yourself Happy

Yes. This is possible. You don't need to be an opera singer or pop music artist. Your voice doesn't have to sound like honey spread over warm toast with a dab of melted butter. You can use singing to help tune up your vagus nerve and give an overall sense of calm to the rest of your body— so, the point is, *do this for you*. Music is powerful, and you can use it to your benefit as long as you can hum.

Here is a quick recap. The PSNS (parasympathetic nervous system) is at its best when you are feeling safe. It slows your heart rate, deepens breathing, propels the digestive system to function so that nutrients get absorbed, and encourages your immune system to thrive. In addition, endorphins, created in your hypothalamus and pituitary gland, get released. These happy chemicals make you feel energized, joyful, and confident. Singing or playing wind instruments (think flute, harmonica, and the like) can help improve your vagal tone and enable you to reap all these benefits.

Making sounds activates the vagus nerve, raising our heart rate variability and vagal tone. This is because the vagus nerve is connected to your vocal cords. In other words, singing can help you improve physical and mental health. So, the next time you feel the urge to sing in the shower— do it! It's even better if you are surrounded by people who make you feel safe, for instance, your family and close friends. Singing together enhances the feeling of contentment and belonging, which has a positive trickling effect on the vagus nerve.

The Power Of Om

In many religious and spiritual practices, chanting is a pathway to the soul and something more significant that offers meaning and hope, the Divine. A mantra is commonly used at the start and the end of a yoga or meditation session. It is known as *Om.* It is a small Sanskrit word with an immense history. According to ancient religions, like Hinduism, *Om* was the first sound of the universe, making it the oldest, most potent, and most powerful sound to exist. In yoga, *Om* (pronounced "*Aum*") represents a space of unison between your body, mind, and spirit. When chanting with others in a yoga class, it is said that it unifies a group and symbolizes the power of comfort and a sense of belonging while maintaining individuality.

Some studies point to its power to encourage relaxation. In one study, chanting Om showed that the vagus nerve was stimulated. In another study, chanting Om for only five minutes boosted activity in the PSNS, which is responsible for relaxation and a peaceful state of mind.

Using this sound doesn't make you a part of the Hindu religion or any other religion. In no way do you need to be religious or spiritual, either. You can use this single-syllable sound to support your vagus nerve. Let your voice guide your mind into a calmer space inside of you.

Chanting Om

The heart of the chant is in an extended exhalation, similar to the 4:8 Breathing Technique. When you exhale as you chant to sounds A-U-M, the controlled rhythmic pace of your breathing in and out leads to that vagus nerve stimulation. Keep a relaxed, soft throat so the sound vibrations from chanting Om resonate in your inner ear and throat. Precisely in the center of your throat, in line with your Adam's apple. This is where your larynx is and where the vagus nerve branches inward. Get a sense of all four sides of your throat when the chant reverberates. Feel the sound in the back, sides, and front throughout the inside of your neck.

1. Set your timer for two minutes (or more when you're ready).

2. Please close your eyes while chanting, making sure to rest them completely.

3. Sit upright with a tall spine, keeping your head in line with the spine.

4. Extend your body upwards as if stretching yourself as tall as you can.

5. Tuck the chin slightly toward your chest to elongate the back of your neck, effectively extending your vagus nerve.

6. Breathe in fully. Take a deep breath through your stomach *via* your nostrils.

7. Breathe out, singing the Om sound (A-U-M) gently, softly, and with intention. Get a sense of your entire throat as you sound out Om (A-U-M)

8. Repeat steps 6 and 7 until the timer goes off.

Music Will Show You the Way

Stephen Porges may have been on to something when he said Disney music is a great way to strengthen and rewire the vagus nerve. Music in itself has both healing and destructive capacities. For example, how often have you been tempted to listen to an extra sob-inducing song when upset about something? Similarly, when you listen to an uplifting piece while already happy, you can reach a higher state of happiness. In the same breath, motivational music exists to help you get things done and get you to believe in yourself.

We already know the vagus nerve lies near the ear, through which we hear music and sounds. When we listen to music, vibrations resonate in our eardrums before traveling through the vagus nerve. Since your vagus nerve is associated with essential functions like taste, digestion, heart rate, and emotional regulation, its activation stimulates the parasympathetic nervous system. It sends a signal saying, "We are safe. It's time to relax."

When you choose the right music for your mind, heart, and body, it feels good. You narrow down to something that resonates in the vagus nerve and triggers a parasympathetic response capable of soothing your body into a calmer state. This is how vibrations help the mind and body— and for some people, Disney music works because it is deeply tied to our nostalgia and roots and positive connections to childhood. There is also another reason it works. The sounds are in the mid-range of the sound frequencies that our ears can hear. Music that uplifts you is always an excellent way to stimulate the vagus nerve, so on those super busy days, always set aside some time for your favorite songs. Mid-range songs are what you're going for. They are the Disney songs, *Imagine* by John Lennon, *Fields of Gold* by Sting, *All of Me* by John Legend, or *Run* by Chasing Cars, to name a few. Use the space at the end of this chapter to write down ten favorite songs you can listen to every other day to strengthen your vagus nerve.

Vagal Nerve Self-Massages

A vagal nerve self-massage is not directly massaging your vagus nerve. Instead, it involves massaging areas near the vagus nerve to stimulate and strengthen your vagal tone. You do this by using gentle, moderate pressure on the space between the sternocleidomastoid and trapezius muscles in the shoulder/neck region and to the muscles below the skull's base with gentle strokes or gentle twisting motions.

The sternocleidomastoid muscles travel down the sides of the neck from the base of the head. They help us rotate our neck and keep the head aligned with the spine. The trapezius muscles are on top of the shoulders, enabling us to move the head, neck, and shoulder blades. Massaging the base of the head, shoulders, and neck has been shown to improve heart rate variability.

Vagus neck self-massage targets essential areas that might produce stress in the body, notably the carotid artery. One carotid artery may be found on each side of the neck. Carotid arteries in good health provide oxygen and blood circulation to the brain and the remainder of the head. When the carotid arteries become constricted or obstructed, the amount of blood and oxygen that can travel through them is reduced. The self-massage induces a relaxation response. Your breathing slows down, and your muscles relax. You might also experience yawning, sighing, warmth, and a heightened sense of hearing, sight, and relaxed speech.

<u>Self-massage method on Ear Tip</u>

The first location on your body that we will focus on stimulating is located on the inside of your ear towards the top. Here's how to find this spot. On the inside of your ear, under the tip of your ear, there is a slight depression. Find and locate this place with your finger. You will find that your fingertip is nestled toward the inside front of your ear towards the top, under the lip of your ear tip, and above a little ridge.

1. Softly and gently massage this point using a circular gentle pressure. Either forwards or backward will work; choose whatever seems most natural for you. This motion is meant to activate your nerve, so do be gentle. Massage this spot for a minute or more if you like.

2. When you are done, pay attention to whether you experience any shifts in sensation or awareness. Breathing patterns may alter for some of you.

3. Repeat steps 1-2 on your other ear.

CALMING YOUR BODY

<u>Self-massage method on Ear Base</u>

The second location on your ear that we will focus on stimulating is also on the inside of your ear at the base. It's adjacent to your ear canal (not in your ear canal) and towards the back of your ear on the inside. Find and locate this place with your finger. You will find that your fingertip is nestled nicely in a little depression, surrounded by the outer ear's cartilage and your inner ear's ridges.

1. Gently and softly massage this point using a circular gentle pressure. Either forwards or backward will work; choose whatever seems most natural for you. This motion is meant to activate your nerve, so do be gentle. Massage this spot for a minute or more if you like.

2. When you are done, pay attention to whether you experience any shifts in breathing, or sensations and awareness.

3. Repeat steps 1-2 on your other ear.

<u>Self-massage method on neck</u>

The third location on your body is your neck. You will need a soft ball that is small to medium-sized for this. This self-massage sequence moves the ball from one side of your neck to the other using a soft, gentle pressure on your neck in order to stimulate your vagus nerve. Be mindful and cautious throughout this self-massage but in particular, once you reach the center of your neck because of the anatomical structures located there.

1. Place this ball on the left side of the upper neck— right under the ear. Your head naturally falls a little back.

2. Very gently use the ball to apply a little pressure to your neck tissue.

3. Gently walk the ball across the neck by twisting the ball slowly as you move the ball. Be gentle with the twist, and move your head in the opposite direction while performing this action. Once you reach the neck's center, be extra cautious because you are in a sensitive space. Keep rotating the ball to the other end of the neck while rotating the head in the opposite direction.

4. When you are done, pay attention to whether you experience any shifts in breathing, or sensations and awareness.

<u>Self-massage method on Foot</u>

The last location on your body is your feet. This exercise is probably something you've done before. And yes, it impacts your vagus nerve, too. So let's do it consciously with awareness.

1. Rotate your ankle, first one way, then the other.

2. Move to rub the sole of your foot with your fingers using short slow strokes

3. Move to gently self-massage and stretch your toes back and forth comfortably. Repeat as you like.

4. Repeat steps 1-3 on your other foot.

5. When you are done, pay attention to whether you experience any shifts in breathing, or sensations and awareness.

Reflections & Notes

Which methods interested me? For what reason(s) did it pique my interest?

I tried out these methods, and this is what I experienced:

Create a vagus nerve playlist: Here are my ten favorite songs in the mid-range of audible sound.

Chapter 7

The Mind-Body Connection

The Brain - Gut Connection

You can eat your way to a better, more vital, healthier vagus nerve by learning about the powerful connection between your brain and your gut. There are routes to optimum health that are as simple as making a conscious decision about what goes into your mouth. Let us begin by attempting to understand what we mean by the "gut-brain axis."

What Is The Gut-Brain Axis?

Do you remember the first time you had a crush on someone or the moment right before you got the results of something important? Conversely, have you experienced a situation where your heart and mind knew something was wrong because *you felt it in your stomach*? Well, the butterflies or the sensation of dread rising within us because we are anxious, nervous, worried, or excited resembles a message from *you to you*. It's not a divine spirit trying to communicate with you. Instead, your gut's divinity is telling you something may or may not happen like you thought or expected.

The gut-brain axis connects your brain's cognitive and emotional zones with your intestinal functions. It is a bridge between your central and enteric nervous systems, responsible for carrying signals from the gut environment to your brain and back to the gut through various immune, endocrine, hormonal and neural links. The axis includes:

- The CNS.

- The brain.

- The spinal cord.

- The autonomic nervous system.

- The enteric nervous system.

- The hypothalamic pituitary adrenal (HPA) axis.

The neurons that make up the enteric nervous system (ENS) are located within the walls of the esophagus, stomach, intestines, pancreas, gallbladder, and pancreato-biliary ducts. The enteric nervous system is a division of the autonomic nervous system, with complete neural circuits that are used to regulate the digestive organs.

The HPA axis is a significant neuroendocrine system that regulates many bodily functions, including digestion and the immune system. It is responsible for controlling how a person reacts to stress.

The term *gut microbiota* refers to the communities of microorganisms, such as archaea and bacteria, found in the digestive systems of insects and vertebrates, including humans. A healthy gut microbiota helps the host with many crucial processes, including nutrition, metabolism, medication, toxic compounds metabolism, mucosal barrier maintenance, immune regulation, and pathogen protection. Therefore, the healthy gut microbiota is instrumental in optimizing the interactions between your brain and your s tomach.

People who experience symptoms of IBS (Irritable Bowel Syndrome) are likely to come down with bouts of anxiety and chronic depression. There is a significant link here, which has to do with the enteric nervous system. While your body cannot write love letters to you, it always tries to communicate and tell you what is in order and what must be improved.

The enteric nervous system's primary responsibility is to control digestion, beginning when you swallow a piece of food. The process continues by releasing different enzymes that break the food down. The final stage is controlling the flow of blood that helps absorb the component nutrients the food is broken down into. Naturally, it communicates with your brain throughout the entire process, which is why there are many emotions surrounding eating.

The enteric nervous system can trigger significant emotional shifts in people already coping with digestive problems like IBS, diarrhea, bloating, constipation, and stomach pains. You will notice a psychosomatic link at play. You often feel an incoming upset stomach when you are most anxious or emotionally vulnerable. It also works the other way around.

Understanding The Importance Of It All

The gut-brain axis operates with a constant information flow between the gut microbiota and the central nervous system. The communication system involves multiple pathways that can be disrupted by stress, environmental irritants, and prolonged antibiotic consumption. Dysbiosis is a condition that signifies a disrupted gut microbiome, the implications of which can be felt in many neurological and mental illnesses. During dysbiosis, the gut-brain axis pathways cannot function as they usually would, which makes the barrier between the CNS and the cardiovascular system porous. In other words, the blood-brain border begins leaking, paving the way for neuroinflammation.

Leaky gut is another name for intestinal permeability. The integrity of the gut's epithelial lining is compromised when we do not have adequate vagus nerve function, correct motility, and proper nutrient absorption. This results in the free circulation of pathogens, poisons, undigested food, and germs throughout the bloodstream, which triggers an inflammatory response from the immune system. Numerous long-term health problems may result from this.

Neuroinflammation has been linked to many illnesses like stroke, Parkinson's, and Alzheimer's. New evidence suggests that disturbances in the gut-brain axis can also lead to unwarranted weight gain because of changes in our metabolism and eating behaviors. A 2020 study suggests disruptions in the gut-brain axis and the communication channels can cause *hangry* "sugar" cravings, making you want to go extra hard on powdered donuts and sugar-loaded drinks.

The five hundred million neurons in the human gut are connected to the brain through nerves. The vagus nerve is among the biggest ones connecting the gastrointestinal tract to the nervous system. It hugely impacts microbiota composition and health and, therefore, inflammation and psychological stress. We tend to think it is anxiety that contributes to stomach problems. However, a group of researchers led by Jay Pasricha, director of the Johns Hopkins Center for Neurogastroenterology, discerns the connection may also exist the other way around. In other words, the food you eat influences your emotional state.

Here are some essential points to remember:

- The gut has about as many nerve cells (or neurons) as the human spinal cord.

- The gut produces about ninety percent of the body's serotonin and fifty percent of dopamine reserves. These potent neurotransmitters significantly affect mood, induce joy and motivation, help the mind stay focused and calm, and act as the body's anti-depressants.

- Our enteric nervous system consists of a plethora of nerve cells that line the muscular walls of the intestines, stomach, rectum, and esophagus. These nerve cells control *peristalsis* or muscle contractions (visualize squeezing the ketchup out of a bottle or toothpaste from a tube) crucial for digestive functions like swallowing, absorption, and bowel movements.

- If the enteric nervous system does not work correctly, it can lead to IBS or gastroparesis. With these conditions, affected individuals could experience repeated counts of diarrhea, painful constipation and piles, and problems with the absorption of food. Additionally, the enteric nerve cells also influence inflammation and immune responses.

- The gut microbiota can make or break your digestive health. And it's pretty challenging to be happy when you are experiencing inflamed diarrhea one day and complete constipation the next. Your mind is constantly in a state of worry and anxiety. Your SNS is perennially telling you that you need to be in a heightened state of frenzy. The only reasoning it offers is *something* is wrong—while the issue hides deep inside your gut ecosystem.

Eight Ways The Vagus Nerve Influences Digestion

Now we know that digestion influences the workings of our nervous system. The next question is, how does the nervous system influence digestion, specifically the vagus nerve?

Firstly, the vagus nerve is responsible for the upkeep of solid food breakdown processes. The body cannot use the food you are consuming. It has to be broken down into functional components— nutrients used by your cells to fuel different functions. The vagus nerve ensures that food is broken down so that we do not experience unpleasant symptoms like bloating, reflux, flatulence, and other forms of gastric imbalance. The vagus nerve is responsible for stimulating saliva formation and secretion. It is no secret that this happens even before you sometimes begin eating. Imagine walking down the road and by a bakery. The fresh smells of cookies, bread, butter, and coffee being poured into pretty cups — these visuals and sensory experiences get the vagus nerve to help saliva secretion, which propels you inside the shop. Once you consume something, the saliva acts as a masticating agent with the aid of enzymes which break the food down before it reaches the esophagus.

Next, the vagus nerve helps stimulate digestive enzymes in your pancreas and bile in your liver. These critical agents break down food so it can continue to pass from the esophagus to the stomach and small and large intestines. After functional components are stored, the remainder is excreted. Optimal vagal tone allows food to be adequately accommodated in the stomach. Enzymes like pepsin and hydrochloric acid break the food down even further. The small intestine is responsible for absorbing the nutrients from our food. After that, the food travels to the large intestine and is eventually expelled through the rectum. The vagus nerve plays a crucial role in the digestive process by stimulating the migrating motor complex in the small intestine, generating a wave-like activity to aid food movement to the large intestine. The vagus nerve slows the process of gastric emptying, so essential nutrients get absorbed instead of excreted to prevent everything we eat from passing through the system too fast.

Finally, the vagus nerve helps you feel full for longer so that your food has time to digest. You don't cycle between periods of ravenous hunger and complete disinterest in food. When your vagus nerve's function and tone are optimal, you will *know* when you are hungry, rather than being influenced by your stress cravings directing you to eat a pizza even though you had a filling lunch half an hour ago. A low vagal tone equals poor emotional regulation, which in turn leaves you vulnerable to the dictates of stress-eating.

Foods To Support Vagus Nerve Healing

At the heart of good health is a stable, wholesome food and nutrition plan. No matter what you do, there is no outrunning a lousy diet. And there's no outrunning expertise, so before you consider supplementing or changing what you are already consuming daily, consult your chosen healthcare professional first.

The research shares that including more prebiotics and probiotics, healthy omega-3 fats, fermented food items, and high-fiber whole grains is an excellent approach to supporting dietary health. A few food groups bear scientific evidence of being great for the gut-brain axis. Let's look at some of them.

- Omega-3 fats are abundant in oily fish, chia seeds, nori, seaweed, perilla oil, and flaxseeds. Also, omega 3's are in Brussels sprouts! So don't dismiss the little green pots of gold. Studies have shown that omega-3 acids can increase good gut bacteria and fight the risk of brain disorders.

- Fermented food items: Edibles like kefir, cheese, yogurt, sauerkraut, sourdough bread, miso, and kimchi contain healthy microbes, including lactic acid bacteria, which have a positive influence on brain activity.

- High-fiber food items like nuts, seeds, leafy greens, whole grains, carrots, beets, broccoli, apples, bananas, and artichokes contain prebiotic fibers that benefit gut bacteria and reduce the prevalence of stress hormones.

- Polyphenol-rich foods like green tea, cocoa, and olive oil are suitable for gut bacteria and may even improve your brain's cognitive capacities.

- Tryptophan-rich food items like cheese, eggs, turkey, peanuts, pumpkin seeds, and whole milk can enhance serotonin levels in your body.

Making any positive dietary change to support your health is not easy; maintaining it may be even more challenging. Even so, it can be done, and it helps your nervous system and specifically supports the health of your vagus nerve. Are you willing?

My Reflections & Notes

Start with tiny and manageable adjustments. Use this section below to consider some simple changes you would like to implement.

What are some simple, realistic changes I can honestly do? What is my reason(s) for making these changes?

Chapter 8

Renewing Your Mind-Body Connection

Creating a Calming Routine

MANY YEARS BACK, 1960 to be specific, Dr. Maxwell Maltz, a renowned plastic surgeon and one of the first recognized writers to claim fame through the self-help genre of writing, found it took his patients three weeks to adjust to their new life and appearances following their surgery. An assumption was born out of this. For a while, most of us would come to believe twenty-one days was enough to internalize an activity so that it would become a habit. The actual average, however, is closer to sixty-six days, which, when you think about it— is just a blip of time compared to the prolonged period of stress your body has already gone through. In this chapter, let's look at ways to support the healing of your vagus nerve and create more wellness. The goal is to gently lean into methods that can become a habit you enjoy because it makes you feel better. Are just over two months of daily activities worth changing to a better routine that's good for your life? It would be an incredible bargain, wouldn't it?

Let's create a straightforward calming routine that can support the health and well-being of your nervous system by helping your vagus nerve. There are a lot of books on creating new habits and routines. My favorite one is Atomic Habits: An Easy & Proven Way to Build Good Habits & Break Bad Ones by James Clear. In the end, however, your approach starts with leaning into doing *one method every day*.

The key takeaways for healing your vagus nerve and helping it so you can help your body, mind, and heart is breathing and movement. This is what begins to turn on the calming "rest and digest" modes of your parasympathetic nervous system. Practicing something daily that incorporates your breathing with a movement is how you begin to tone up your vagus nerve and tell your nervous system that you are safe. And it doesn't take much. It takes a few minutes a few times a day to begin. And remember to speak with your health professional(s) before you make any health-related changes.

Create a Simple Calming Routine

Go back to the reflections you wrote throughout the book. Go back and review the methods in this book. Take more than a moment to read, scan and absorb what you wrote and which exercises interested you.

1. Make a short list of the methods you'd like to try.

2. Take a look at the list of methods you wrote down.

3. Pick 1 item you can realistically do every day for a couple of minutes, 2-3 times a day.

4. Pick 1 - 3 times a day you can do it realistically. Is it before or after a meal? When do you take a restroom break? When is an easy time?

5. Set the alarm for these times if this helps.

6. Commit yourself to doing this every day. Start with one day. Then go for two days. Then go for three days.

7. Begin today. Begin right now.

A word about exercise

Movement is breathing. Breathing is movement. These are the keys to stimulating your vagus nerve and improving your vagal tone. Exercise means moving and living. It's probably no surprise that exercise is a powerful way to support your vagal tone and experience your nervous system responding with relaxation. The effects of it can carry on not only into your waking hours but also your sleep.

Moderate-intensity activities will be your best choice for improving your HRV and vagal tone. Studies have shown that exercise strengthens HRV; over twelve months, a moderate exercise routine positively impacted children with low HRV.

Moderate intensity is the way to go. Your focus should be on exertion levels that make you feel good without inducing tears and curses because everything hurts. You can make almost any movement activity you like into moderately intense exercise. You'll know you're doing something at this level when you can still speak, but singing a song is not an option. At this point, your heart rate is raised, and you are breaking a sweat.

Keep in mind moderate intensity is different for everyone. Something that's moderate intensity for you may be different for me. You may find running is a moderately intense activity. I may discover brisk walking works better as moderately intense exercise. There is a self-respect element here. Respect where your body is. You may have enjoyed doing jump rope, and now your knees are saying, "No, let's find something else."

Here are further tips to make this your own:

- Identify patterns that are sabotaging your good intentions. Plan consciously so your simple calming routine will help you.

- Set realistic goals. Remember that the timeline is only doable if it does not break you physically and emotionally. You are not in a war; you are on a beautiful journey. Enjoy it.

- Any of the methods in this book can be done anywhere, but why not create a little space in your office and a corner of your home to do this? Can you keep it simple? For example, choose a place in the room where you place a chair in front of a window. Go there.

- Maximize your time with healthful hobbies. Try new exercises, participate in particular activities, or socialize with friends and family.

- Track your progress. Track how activities will assist you in concentrating and catch slip-ups, but no need to judge. Establish awareness and prepare yourself differently next time.

- If your surroundings include too much temptation, remove them from your immediate reach. Addicting items can consist of anything that will take you away from your commitment. This includes bottles of alcohol, unhealthy food items, or anything that feels like quick comfort. If it's too easy, it's likely not worth having.

- Ask for support. Be proud of yourself for choosing to go on this journey. People who love you will be just as pleased to help and cheer you on. Let them know. Find like-minded others, perhaps a support group who will have your back.

- Choose progress over perfection. Be patient. It takes time to progress, and sometimes you have setbacks— these are nothing but tools that will help you learn.

- Give yourself a treat from time to time. Treat yourself when you have accomplished a modest objective or reached a significant milestone. You could go for a relaxing, professional massage, read an excellent book, cook a beautiful meal or get some alone time.

- Keep things light and fun, and be gentle with yourself.

- Dream about your future. Visualize the life you have always wanted coming closer and closer; one day, it just will.

You now know how to create a simple calming routine. Create it and begin using it to lean into a healthier habit that will benefit your vagus nerve and help you relieve stress, restore ease, and renew your body-mind connection.

My Reflections & Notes

Leave a 1-Click Review

Hello. Did you enjoy reading this book?

Would you please leave a review? Your words may help guide potential readers who might benefit from learning more about their vagus nerve. Feeling better is all about the small changes that lead to more significant outcomes. Make a change in your life and help others increase the potential of making a positive change in theirs.

Thank you in advance if you enjoyed this book and decided to take just 60 seconds to write a brief review on Amazon, even if it's just a few sentences. I appreciate it!

>>>>>> **Click here to leave a quick review** <<<<<<

Conclusion

We are now at the end of our journey together. But, like all endings, this one, too, is nothing but a beginning—a beginning to another way of building health. Living life more fully, feeling more at ease in your body, calmer in your mind, and more open in your heart, while being connected to those you love is a natural desire—a basic human need. Being a better person includes improving care for yourself and learning to bounce back from challenges. Connecting more consciously with your body, mind, heart, and spirit can be a stepping stone to feeling safer and more secure. From here, connecting with loved ones and others feels safer, too. It begins with you, at home in your own body.

Are you ready to take some manageable, straightforward steps to help you feel good in your body and strengthen your mind-body connection? Stimulating the vagus nerve can be part of your journey to better health and can support health issues that may have held you captive. This is because the vagus nerve acts as a hub, coordinating several communication routes that assist in the various parts of your body working together. For example, constant communication occurs between the brain, heart, stomach, and spinal cord. In this symphony, the vagus nerve plays the conductor role, instructing the brain to secrete neurotransmitters and substances to control many responses like stress, coordinating reactions, limiting inflammation, and creating calm.

You already know how your world is when these automatic autonomic responses make you feel stressed out. It's hard to enjoy a meal that you typically would because your stomach is upset. A cup of tea would usually stabilize you, but today, it makes you wiry and jittery. A phone call and a simple "how are you?" from your mother elicits an irritable, grumpy response, and inside, you think about how she is interfering in your life—although deep down, the truth is she is only looking out for you because she loves you.

During these times, you can forget to breathe when your body produces large amounts of stress and takes over your senses moving into a fight, flight, or freeze way of responding. Holding the breath activates stress responses and can lead to increased nervousness. So, remember that whenever you practice a method, breathe, breathe, breathe. When you focus on the rhythm of your breathing regularly, you may even begin to change your mind about a stressor. You may even begin to move into accepting it just as it is. In this way, you can go back to enjoying your meal and tea, and when your mom calls, you are very happy to hear her voice.

Stimulating your vagus nerve may also help improve the overall health of your nervous system, especially your autonomic nervous system. A sound autonomic nervous system relaxes your body, calms your thoughts and stabilizes your emotions. Emotional stability strengthens bonds with yourself and others. Good physical health is greatly supported by a vagus nerve in good working order. Consciously working together with your nervous system is powerful. When your nervous system, especially your vagus nerve, feels supported by your deliberate, conscious attention, your nervous system remembers and helps you, too. You will be better equipped to recover from your life's stressors and become stronger. You can support your nervous system by learning and working with it. Vagus nerve healing can be a way for you to feel more vital and enjoy your day-to-day life again so you can move forward with the life you aspire to and, hopefully with greater ease.

It is stressful to have an acute or chronic health challenge or condition. You can have limited physical and mental energy to do things. This book offered clear, uncomplicated fundamental evidence-based information on why restoring the health of your vagus nerve may be an essential component of your healing path. On this journey, you learned how to use these gentle, non-invasive methods to complement your healthcare provider's recommendations, which can help you become a little more settled in your body, and calm in your mind and heart so you can feel more comfortable in your skin. In truth, these methods appear deceptively simple, yet they are mighty. This book is aimed at the basics around strategies that help your mind and body feel connected so you feel more at ease. We discussed several ways to stimulate your vagus nerve and support your vagal tone by using breathing, meditation, food, and exercise. Your breathing and movement are key to relieving stress, restoring ease, and renewing yourself. The most wholesome process you can do for you when it comes to your vagus nerve is prolonged, deep breathing. The biggest cheerleader you can have is your breath; that rise and fall can be a force to move you onward and upward. Breathing exercises help shift your focus and help your nervous system shift to make you feel more relief and, over time, enhance better outcomes for your overall health.

There is no magic wand here. It takes work. As you continue on your journey to better health and wellness, may your path lead you to rediscover life's new joys. Sweet mornings and quiet nights can happen more regularly if you are patient and consistent. The work described in this book can be done in a relatively short amount of time but don't let that fool you. These methods are used by many people and have the backing of research. These techniques have improved my life living with a chronic condition. They are the core of what I do to relieve stress and renew myself. These methods keep a smile on my face and help my body, mind, heart, and spirit feel genuinely good, calm, and well. The truth is, I'm thriving, not surviving. Make a commitment to feel better for the good of your own heart, mind, body, and spirit. Now that you have this new information, all that remains is the doing of it – practicing it. Practicing is a long-term commitment. There will be setbacks. Accept them. There will be progress. Let the wins fuel your health journey. Take more deep breaths and be patient with yourself, then re-commit. Pick yourself up and move forward. Your family, friends, and loved ones are rooting for you.

Your nervous system is a thriving, intelligent aspect of who you are, waiting to love you back just as you deserve. I hope the information in this book helps you become more comfortable with being yourself in your own skin. I hope you create healthier ways to cope with your stress response and become more resilient to the stressors in your life. And I sincerely hope you grow into feeling a stronger connection to what has meaning, to what you value, and a better sense of belonging to yourself, your family, friends, loved ones, and even this world. May you move forward to a better level of wellness, manage your stress in new ways, and experience more calm in y our life.

Now, all that remains to relieve your stress, restore more ease, and renew your mind-body connection is to take several deep conscious breaths and begin.

A Free Gift for You, Dear Reader

Thank you for your purchase. Use this QR code to download the Guide to Stress Management workbook. Or click this link. You'll find:

- Essentials for stress management and stress relief.

- Exercises that help you figure out what holds you back from relieving your stress.

- Prompts for journaling so you can hear your inner wisdom better.

- Easy ways of making simple changes that can help you create better stress management habits.

Endnotes

Introduction

American Psychological Association. (2022, October). *Stress in america 2022: Concerned for the future, beset by inflation*. American Psychological Association. Retrieved December 11, 2022, from https://www.apa.org/news/press/releases/stress/2022/concerned-future-inflation

Breit S, Kupferberg A, Rogler G and Hasler G (2018) Vagus Nerve as Modulator of the Brain–Gut Axis in Psychiatric and Inflammatory Disorders. *Front. Psychiatry* 9:44. Retrieved September 5, 2022, from doi: 10.3389/fpsyt.2018.00044

Knight, K. (2021). 'Fight or flight' dates back to ancient ancestors. *Journal of Experimental Biology*, *224*(11). Retrieved September 5, 2022, from https://doi.org/10.1242/jeb.242837

Chapter 1

Cornell Health Stress Management. (2011, June 16). *Understanding and Managing Stress at Cornell*. Understanding-Managing-Stress.pdf. Retrieved September 27, 2022, from https://health.cornell.edu/sites/health/files/pdf-library/understanding-managing-stress.pdf

Dale HH, Feldberg W. The chemical transmitter of vagus effects to the stomach. J Physiol. 1934 Jun 9;81(3):320-34. Retrieved September 27, 2022, from https://www.ncbi.nlm.nih.gov/pmc/articles/PMC1394148/

Gentry, J. E., & Block, I. K. (2016). *Forward facing trauma therapy: Healing the moral wound.* Compassion Unlimited. https://forward-facing.com/forward-facing-trauma-therapy/

Kolacz, J., & Porges, S. W. (2018). Chronic Diffuse Pain and Functional Gastrointestinal Disorders After Traumatic Stress: Pathophysiology Through a Polyvagal Perspective. *Frontiers in Medicine, 5.* Retrieved September 27, 2022, from https://doi.org/10.3389/fmed.2018.00145

Metro Health & Medical Preparedness Coalition, & Masa Consulting. (2020, August 17). *Building resilience: One step at a time the stress continuum model.* metrohealthready.org. Retrieved September 5, 2022, from https://metrohealthready.org/wp-content/uploads/2020/08/Stress-Continuum-One-Page-MetroCoalition.pdf

Nagoski, E., & Nagoski, A. (2021, June 21). *Feeling emotionally exhausted? 6 things you can do to release your stress.* Retrieved September 5, 2022, from https://Ideas.Ted.Com/Emotionally-Exhausted-Burnout-Completing-Stress-Response-Cycle/

Porges, E. C., Woods, A. J., Edden, R. A., Puts, N. A., Harris, A. D., Chen, H., ... & Cohen, R. A. (2017). Frontal gamma-aminobutyric acid concentrations are associated with cognitive performance in older adults. *Biological Psychiatry: Cognitive Neuroscience and Neuroimaging, 2*(1), 38-44. Retrieved September 6, 2022, from https://pubmed.ncbi.nlm.nih.gov/28217759/

Porges, S. W. (2011). *The polyvagal theory: Neurophysiological foundations of emotions, attachment, communication, and self-regulation (Norton Series on Interpersonal Neurobiology).* WW Norton & Company. https://www.ncbi.nlm.nih.gov/pmc/articles/PMC3490536/

Porges, S. (2017, November 3). *The polyvagal theory: The new science of safety and trauma*. The Polyvagal Theory: The New Science of Safety and Trauma. Retrieved September 27, 2022, from https://www.youtube.com/watch?v=br8-qebjIgs

Scott, E. (2022, May 23). *What is chronic stress?* Verywell Mind. Retrieved September 27, 2022, from https://www.verywellmind.com/chronic-stress-3145104

Wagner, D. (2016, June 27). *Polyvagal theory in practice*. Polyvagal Theory in Practice. Retrieved November 12, 2022, from https://ct.counseling.org/2016/06/polyvagal-theory-practice/

Whitlock, J. (2021, March 12). *Assess your stress–where are you on the stress continuum?* Assess Your Stress–Where Are You on the Stress Continuum? Retrieved September 27, 2022, from https://accelerate.uofuhealth.utah.edu/resilience/assess-your-stress-where-are-you-on-the-stress-continuum

Windhorse IMH. (2020, January 10). *Being polyvagal: The polyvagal theory explained*. Windhorse Integrative Mental Health. Retrieved September 27, 2022, from https://www.windhorseimh.org/being-polyvagal-the-polyvagal-theory-explained/

Yaribeygi, H., Panahi, Y., Sahraei, H., Johnston, T. P., & Sahebkar, A. (2017). The impact of stress on body function: A review. *EXCLI Journal, 16*, 1057–1072. Retrieved September 6, 2022, from https://doi.org/10.17179/excli2017-480

Chapter 2: You've Got Some Nerve

Byrne, M. (2022, July 22). *Vagus nerve*. Vagus Nerve. Retrieved November 12, 2022, from https://www.kenhub.com/en/library/anatomy/the-vagus-nerve

Cavanagh, J. B. (1969). Toxic substances and the nervous system. *British medical bulletin*, *25*(3), 268-273. Retrieved October 15, 2022, from https://doi.org/10.1093/oxfordjournals.bmb.a070716

Cleveland Clinic, M. P. (2020, May 12). *Nervous system: What it is, types, symptoms*. Cleveland Clinic. Retrieved September 5, 2022, from https://my.clevelandclinic.org/health/articles/21202-nervous-system

Cleveland Clinic. (2022, October 14). *Peripheral neuropathy: What it is, symptoms & treatment*. Cleveland Clinic. Retrieved October 15, 2022, from https://my.clevelandclinic.org/health/diseases/14737-peripheral-neuropathy

Discovery Health Writers (2008, September 10). The brain and mental health. Retrieved September 10, 2022, from https://health.howstuffworks.com/human-body/systems/nervous-system/brain-and-mental-health.htm

Finsterer J, Grisold W. Disorders of the lower cranial nerves. J Neurosci Rural Pract. 2015 Jul-Sep;6(3):377-91. Retrieved October 15, 2022, from doi: 10.4103/0976-3147.158768. PMID: 26167022; PMCID: PMC4481793.

Flint Rehab. (2022, September 20). *Neuropathy after stroke: Understanding & treating the pain*. Flint Rehab. Retrieved November 12, 2022, from https://www.flintrehab.com/neuropathy-after-stroke/

Han, S., Seladi-Schulman, J., & Hobbs, H. (2022, May 5). *The 12 cranial nerves*. Healthline. Retrieved November 12, 2022, from https://www.healthline.com/health/12-cranial-nerves#iii-oculomotor-nerve

Instituto Clavel. (2020, January 6). *The human nervous system: Parts and main functions*. The human nervous system: parts and main function. Retrieved November 12, 2022, from https://www.institutoclavel.com/en/the-human-nervous-system-parts-and-main-functions

Li, F., He, T., Xu, Q., Lin, L.-T., Li, H., Liu, Y., Shi, G.-X., & Liu, C.-Z. (2015). What is the Acupoint? A preliminary review of Acupoints.

Pain Medicine, *16*(10), 1905–1915. Retrieved October 15, 2022, from https://doi.org/10.1111/pme.12761

Penn Medicine. (2022). Cranial Nerve Disorders. Retrieved September 5, 2022, from https://www.pennmedicine.org/for-patients-and-visitors/find-a-program-or-service/neurosurgery/cranial-nerve-disorders/conditions-and-diagnosis

Peripheral Neuropathy. (2022) Retrieved October 15, 2022, from https://Www.Mayoclinic.Org/Diseases-Conditions/Peripheral-Neuropathy/Symptoms-Causes/Syc-20352061

Peters A. The Effects of Normal Aging on Nerve Fibers and Neuroglia in the Central Nervous System. In: *Riddle DR, editor. Brain Aging: Models, Methods, and Mechanisms. Boca Raton* (FL): CRC Press/Taylor & Francis; 2007. Chapter 5. Retrieved October 15, 2022, from https://www.ncbi.nlm.nih.gov/books/NBK3873/

Pietrangelo, A. (2022, May 31). *Why Am I Experiencing Numbness and Tingling?* Retrieved October 15, 2022, from https://Www.Healthline.Com/Health/Numbness-and-Tingling

Chapter 3: Inner Strength

Beusekom, M. (2022, February 14). *Scientists propose cause of symptoms, treatment for long COVID-19.* CIDRAP; University of Minnesota. Retrieved November 12, 2022 from https://www.cidrap.umn.edu/news-perspective/2022/02/scientists-propose-cause-symptoms-treatment-long-covid-19

Beusekom, M. (2022, November 11). *Long recovery, brain damage, effect of stressors with Long Covid.* UMN CIDRAP . Retrieved November 12, 2022 from https://www.cidrap.umn.edu/news-perspective/2022/11/long-recovery-brain-damage-effect-stressors-long-covid

Bottaro, A. (2022, January 26). *Connection between Lyme Disease & the vagus nerve*. Lyme Time. Retrieved November 12, 2022, from https://lyme-time.com/2022/02/07/connection-between-lyme-disease-vagus-nerve/

Breit S, Kupferberg A, Rogler G and Hasler G (2018) Vagus Nerve as Modulator of the Brain–Gut Axis in Psychiatric and Inflammatory Disorders. *Front. Psychiatry* 9:44. Retrieved November 13, 2022 from https://doi: 10.3389/fpsyt.2018.00044

Chen, J.-L., Chiu, H.-W., Tseng, Y.-J., & Chu, W.-C. (2006). Hyperthyroidism is characterized by both increased sympathetic and decreased vagal modulation of heart rate: evidence from spectral analysis of heart rate variability. *Clinical Endocrinology*, *64*(6), 611–616. Retrieved November 13, 2022 from

https://doi.org/10.1111/j.1365-2265.2006.02514.x

de Meersman, R. E. (1993). Heart rate variability and aerobic fitness. *American Heart Journal*, *125*(3), 726–731. Retrieved November 13, 2022 from

https://pubmed.ncbi.nlm.nih.gov/8438702/

Gierthmühlen, M., & Plachta, D. T. T. (2016). Effect of selective vagal nerve stimulation on blood pressure, heart rate and respiratory rate in rats under metoprolol medication. *Hypertension Research*, *39*(2), 79–87. Retrieved November 14, 2022 from

https://doi.org/10.1038/hr.2015.122

Grassi, G., Mark, A., & Esler, M. (2015). The Sympathetic Nervous System Alterations in Human Hypertension. *Circulation Research*, *116*(6), 976–990. Retrieved November 14, 2022 from

https://doi.org/10.1161/CIRCRESAHA.116.303604

Henderson, E. (2022, February 13). *Study points to vagus nerve dysfunction as a central pathophysiological feature of Long Covid*. News Medical Life Sciences. Retrieved September 5, 2022, from https://www.news-medical.net/news/20220212/Study-points-to-vagus

-nerve-dysfunction-as-a-central-pathophysiological-feature-of-long-COVID.aspx

Lladós, G., & Mateu, L. (2022). *Pilot study suggests long COVID could be linked to the effects of SARS-CoV-2 on the vagus nerve*. Retrieved September 5, 2022, from https://www.news-medical.net/news/20220212/Study-points-to-vagus-nerve-dysfunction-as-a-central-pathophysiological-feature-of-long-COVID.aspx

Malbert, C.-H. (2018). Could vagus nerve stimulation have a role in the treatment of diabetes? *Bioelectronics in Medicine*, *1*(1), 13–15. Retrieved September 5, 2022, from https://doi.org/10.2217/bem-2017-0008

Mariotti A. (2015). The effects of chronic stress on health: new insights into the molecular mechanisms of brain-body communication. *Future science* OA, 1(3), FSO23. Retrieved September 5, 2022, from https://doi.org/10.4155/fso.15.21

Pavlov, V. A., & Tracey, K. J. (2012). The vagus nerve and the inflammatory reflex—linking immunity and metabolism. *Nature Reviews Endocrinology*, *8*(12), 743–754. Retrieved September 5, 2022, from https://doi.org/10.1038/nrendo.2012.189

Puri, B. K., Shah, M., Monro, J. A., Kingston, M. C., & Julu, P. O. (2014). Respiratory modulation of cardiac vagal tone in Lyme disease. *World journal of cardiology*, 6(6), 502–506. Retrieved September 5, 2022, from https://doi.org/10.4330/wjc.v6.i6.502

Vagus Nerve Dysfunction Disorders. (2022). Retrieved September 5, 2022, from https://www.Flatironsintegrative.Com/Vagus-Nerve-Index

Chapter 4: Calming your mind

Bunn, T. (2020, April 1). *That advice on calming yourself isn't working, is it?* Psychology Today. Retrieved September 18,

2022 from https://www.psychologytoday.com/us/blog/conquer-fear-flying/202004/advice-calming-yourself-isnt-working-is-it

Creswell, J. D., Taren, A. A., Lindsay, E. K., Greco, C. M., Gianaros, P. J., Fairgrieve, A., Marsland, A. L., Brown, K. W., Way, B. M., Rosen, R. K., & Ferris, J. L. (2016). Alterations in Resting-State Functional Connectivity Link Mindfulness Meditation With Reduced Interleukin-6: A Randomized Controlled Trial. *Biological Psychiatry*, *80*(1), 53–61. Retrieved September 18, 2022 from https://doi.org/10.1016/j.biopsych.2016.01.008

de Couck, M., Caers, R., Musch, L., Fliegauf, J., Giangreco, A., & Gidron, Y. (2019). How breathing can help you make better decisions: Two studies on the effects of breathing patterns on heart rate variability and decision-making in business cases. *International Journal of Psychophysiology*, *139*, 1–9. Retrieved September 18, 2022 from https://doi.org/10.1016/j.ijpsycho.2019.02.011

Fang, J., Rong, P., Hong, Y., Fan, Y., Liu, J., Wang, H., Zhang, G., Chen, X., Shi, S., Wang, L., Liu, R., Hwang, J., Li, Z., Tao, J., Wang, Y., Zhu, B., & Kong, J. (2016). Transcutaneous Vagus Nerve Stimulation Modulates Default Mode Network in Major Depressive Disorder. *Biological Psychiatry*, *79*(4), 266–273. Retrieved September 18, 2022 from https://pubmed.ncbi.nlm.nih.gov/25963932/

Fowler, P. (2022, January 17). *Breathing Techniques for Stress Relief*. Retrieved September 18, 2022 from https://www.Webmd.Com/Balance/Stress-Management/Stress-Relief-Breathing-Techniques

Gelles, D. (2022). *How to Meditate*. Retrieved September 18, 2022 from https://www.nytimes.com/guides/well/how-to-meditate

Gerritsen, R. J. S., & Band, G. P. H. (2018). Breath of Life: The Respiratory Vagal Stimulation Model of Contemplative Activity. *Frontiers in Human Neuroscience*, *12*. Retrieved September 18, 2022 from https://doi.org/10.3389/fnhum.2018.00397

Vagus nerve stimulation. (2022). Retrieved September 18, 2022 from https://www.wimhofmethod.com/Vagus-Nerve-Stimulation

Chapter 5: Biofeedback

Cherry, K. (2021, July 11). *What is biofeedback?* Verywell Mind. Retrieved September 9, 2022, from https://www.verywellmind.com/what-is-biofeedback-2794875

Frank, D. L., Khorshid, L., Kiffer, J. F., Moravec, C. S., & McKee, M. G. (2010). Biofeedback in medicine: who, when, why and how? *Mental health in family medicine*, 7(2), 85–91. September 9, 2022, from https://www.ncbi.nlm.nih.gov/pmc/articles/PMC2939454/

Mayo Clinic Staff. (2021, March 18). *Biofeedback*. Mayo Clinic. Retrieved September 9, 2022, from September 9, 2022, from https://www.mayoclinic.org/tests-procedures/biofeedback/about/pac-20384664

Wilson, S., & Ratini, M. (2020, September 16). *Biofeedback therapy: Uses and benefits*. WebMD. Retrieved September 9, 2022, from https://www.webmd.com/pain-management/biofeedback-therapy-uses-benefits

Chapter 6: Calming your body

Dalton, C. (2021, May 31). *Music for the soul*. Brisbane City Psychologists. Retrieved November 12, 2022, from https://www.brisbanecitypsychologist.com.au/music-for-the-soul-by-clinical-psychologist-cherie-dalton/

Hui. (2022, February 25). *Can Stimulating the Vagus Nerve Actually Transform Your Health?* Verywell Health. Retrieved October 4, 2022, from https://www.verywellhealth.com/vagus-nerve-health-conditions-5219941

Inbaraj, G., Rao, R. M., Ram, A., Bayari, S. K., Belur, S., Prathyusha, P. v, Sathyaprabha, T. N., & Udupa, K. (2022). Immediate Effects of OM Chanting on Heart Rate Variability Measures Compared Between Experienced and Inexperienced Yoga Practitioners.

International Journal of Yoga, *15*(1), 52–58. October 4, 2022, from https://pubmed.ncbi.nlm.nih.gov/35444369/

Kalyani, B. G., Venkatasubramanian, G., Arasappa, R., Rao, N., Kalmady, S., Behere, R., Rao, H., & Vasudev, M. (2011). Neuro Hemodynamic correlates of 'OM' chanting: A pilot functional magnetic resonance i maging study. *International Journal of Yoga*, *4*(1), 3. October 4, 2022, from https://doi.org/10.4103/0973-6131.78171

LePera, N. (2021, July 3). *How to do a vagus nerve massage*. How to do a Vagus Nerve Massage by The Holistic Psychologist. Retrieved November 19, 2022, from https://www.youtube.com/watch?v=9uZ1rnKF5DU

Missimer, A. (2021, June 9). *Vagus nerve hack: Neck release*. The Vagus Nerve hack Neck Release. Retrieved November 19, 2022, from https://t hemovementparadigm.com/vagus-nerve-hack-neck-release

Pierson, C. (2020, June 14). *Thai Foot Massage & the vagus nerve*. The Float Spa. Retrieved November 19, 2022, from https://www.thefloatspa .co.uk/thai-foot-massage-vagus-nerve/

Porges, S. (2017, November 3). *The polyvagal theory: The new science of safety and trauma*. The Polyvagal Theory: The New Science of Safety and Trauma. Retrieved September 27, 2022, from https://www.youtube.co m/watch?v=br8-qebjIgs

S. K., Belur, S., Prathyusha, P. V., ... & Udupa, K. (2022). Immediate effects of OM chanting on heart rate variability measures compared between experienced and inexperienced yoga practitioners. *International Journal of Yoga*, *15*(1), 52. October 4, 2022, from https://pubmed.ncbi.nlm.nih.gov/35444369/

Stones, S. (2017, November 14). *The Importance of Om & How To Chant It Effectively*. October 4, 2022, from https://samatas-tones.com/blogs/blog/the-importance-of-om

Chapter 7: Mind-Body Connection

Bliss, E. S., & Whiteside, E. (2017). The Gut-Brain Axis, the Human Gut Microbiota and Their Integration in the Development of Obesity. *Frontiers in Physiology*. October 4, 2022, from https://doi.org/10.3389/fphys.2018.00900

Brickman, A. M., Khan, U. A., Provenzano, F. A., Yeung, L. K., Suzuki, W., Schroeter, H., Wall, M., Sloan, R. P., & Small, S. A. (2014). Enhancing dentate gyrus function with dietary flavanols improves cognition in older adults. *Nature neuroscience*, *17*(12), 1798–1803. October 4, 2022, from https://doi.org/10.1038/nn.3850

Hayek, N. (2013). Chocolate, gut microbiota, and human health. *Frontiers in Pharmacology*, *4*. October 4, 2022, from https://doi.org/10.3389/fphar.2013.00011

Jenkins, T., Nguyen, J., Polglaze, K., & Bertrand, P. (2016). Influence of Tryptophan and Serotonin on Mood and Cognition with a Possible Role of the Gut-Brain Axis. *Nutrients*, *8*(1), 56. October 4, 2022, from https://doi.org/10.3390/nu8010056

Johns Hopkins Medicine. (2012, December 12). *Inside tract - it's high time for the gut-brain*. Johns Hopkins Medicine. Retrieved September 27, 2022, from https://www.hopkinsmedicine.org/news/publications/inside_tract/inside_tract_fall_2012/its_high_time_for_the_gut_brain

Menni, C., Zierer, J., Pallister, T., Jackson, M. A., Long, T., Mohney, R. P., Steves, C. J., Spector, T. D., & Valdes, A. M. (2017). Omega-3 fatty acids correlate with gut microbiome diversity and production of N-carbamylglutamate in middle aged and elderly women. *Scientific Reports*, *7*(1), 11079. September 27, 2022, from https://doi.org/10.1038/s41598-017-10382-2

Mocking, R. J. T., Harmsen, I., Assies, J., Koeter, M. W. J., Ruhé, H. G., & Schene, A. H. (2016). Meta-analysis and meta-regression of omega-3 polyunsaturated fatty acid supplementation for major depressive disorder. *Translational Psychiatry, 6*(3), e756–e756. September 27, 2022, from https://doi.org/10.1038/tp.2016.29

Murray, E. (2022, February 1). *The Gut-Brain Axis, Simplified* . September 27, 2022, from https://thechangingroom.Blog/2022/02/01/the-Gut-Brain-Axis-Somewhat-Simplified/

Robertson, R. C., Seira Oriach, C., Murphy, K., Moloney, G. M., Cryan, J. F., Dinan, T. G., Paul Ross, R., & Stanton, C. (2017). Omega-3 polyunsaturated fatty acids critically regulate behavior and gut microbiota development in adolescence and adulthood. *Brain, Behavior, and Immunity, 59*, 21–37. September 27, 2022, from https://doi.org/10.1016/j.bbi.2016.07.145

Rutsch, A., Kantsjö, J. B., & Ronchi, F. (2020). The Gut-Brain Axis: How Microbiota and Host Inflammasome Influence Brain Physiology and Pathology. *Frontiers in Immunology, 11*. September 27, 2022, from https://doi.org/10.3389/fimmu.2020.604179

Schmidt, K., Cowen, P. J., Harmer, C. J., Tzortzis, G., Errington, S., & Burnet, P. W. J. (2015). Prebiotic intake reduces the waking cortisol response and alters emotional bias in healthy volunteers. *Psychopharmacology, 232*(10), 1793–1801. September 27, 2022, from https://doi.org/10.1007/s00213-014-3810-0

Tan, H. E., Sisti, A. C., Jin, H., Vignovich, M., Villavicencio, M., Tsang, K. S., ... & Zuker, C. S. (2020). The gut–brain axis mediates sugar preference. *Nature, 580*(7804), 511-516. September 27, 2022, from https://pubmed.ncbi.nlm.nih.gov/32322067/

Tillisch, K., Labus, J., Kilpatrick, L., Jiang, Z., Stains, J., Ebrat, B., Guyonnet, D., Legrain–Raspaud, S., Trotin, B., Naliboff, B., & Mayer, E. A. (2013). Consumption of Fermented Milk Product With Probiotic Modulates Brain Activity. *Gastroenterology, 144*(7), 1394-1401.e4. September 27, 2022, from https://doi.org/10.1053/j.gastro.2013.02.043

Vagus Nerve: Gastroparesis, Vagus Nerve Stimulation & Syncope. (n.d.). Cleveland Clinic. Retrieved October 4, 2022, from https://my.clevelandclinic.org/health/body/22279-vagus-nerve

Chapter 8: Renew your Mind-Body Connection

Centers for Disease Control and Prevention. (2022, June 2). *How much physical activity do adults need?* Centers for Disease Control and Prevention. Retrieved October 19, 2022, from https://www.cdc.gov/physicalactivity/basics/adults/index.htm

Goldsmith, R. L., Bigger, J. T., Steinman, R. C., & Fleiss, J. L. (1992). Comparison of 24-hour parasympathetic activity in endurance-trained and untrained young men. *Journal of the American College of Cardiology, 20*(3), 552–558. September 27, 2022, from https://doi.org/10.1016/0735-1097(92)90007-A

Moritani, T., Hamada, T., Kimura, T., & Nagai, N. (2004). Moderate physical exercise increases cardiac autonomic nervous system activity in children with low heart rate variability. *Child's Nervous System, 20*(4), 209–214. September 27, 2022, from https://doi.org/10.1007/s00381-004-0915-5

Seravalle, G., Mancia, G., & Grassi, G. (2018). Sympathetic Nervous System, Sleep, and Hypertension. *Current Hypertension Reports, 20*(9), 74. September 27, 2022, from https://doi.org/10.1007/s11906-018-0874-y

Resources

Helpful Books & Organizations

- The Pocket Guide to the Polyvagal Theory: The Transformative Power of Feeling Safe by Stephen W. Porges, Ph.D.

- Atomic Habits: An Easy & Proven Way to Build Good Habits & Break Bad Ones by James Clear

- The Polyvagal Institute: https://www.polyvagalinstitute.org/mission-and-team

- National Center for PTSD: https://www.ptsd.va.gov/

Acknowledgments

I appreciate and am thankful for the smiling support of the following people. To my AIA family, especially Juan, Brian, Cody, Kim, Churchill, and the Twins: thank you for your inspiration, guidance, and constructive feedback. To my Cosmic Ally, Tony, my Cosmic Cousins, and Sweet Spot Tribes: thank you for your energizing support, problem-solving skills, generosity, and masterful minds. To my Crown Jewels & Sunray Tribes: thank you for your positivity and soul support. To my healing sisters, Kate, Kathleen, and Sophie: thank you for your magnetic fields. And to my dear loving family, who help me grow and realize dreams every day. I am grateful.

About The Author
Ione Goodhart

Ione Goodhart writes about stress management, mind-body methods, and how making small, simple lifestyle changes can make a difference when facing and recovering from health challenges and concerns. In her free time, Ione enjoys yoga, meditation, and having fun with her loved ones. She lives in Connecticut with her family.

Made in the USA
Monee, IL
19 May 2023